Hans Ibelings

20th Century Urban Design in the Netherlands

NAi Publishers

Rotterdam

Introduction

20th Century Urban Design in the Netherlands **is intended to offer readers a clearly organized introduction to the history of Dutch urban design. Each of the ten chapters surveys the output of a single decade in words and, above all, in pictures. Urban design is a wide field encompassing not just the actual drawing up of urban development plans but also theories of urban design and spatial planning, as well as the relevant national and local government policy. All of these aspects are dealt with in this book but the emphasis is less on the abstract, cartographic picture than on the concrete street-level picture. The point of departure is a desire to shed light on how the Dutch built environment has changed over the course of the century and what the underlying ideas and strengths have been. Both exception and rule are covered. Alongside acknowledged highlights of Dutch twentieth-century urban design are the more everyday products of the prevailing ideas of designers, government and politicians.**

Several trends can be discerned in twentieth-century Dutch urban design, most notably the ongoing urbanization and the growing number of planning instruments available to practitioners. Over the course of the last hundred years, spatial planning in the Netherlands has also become increasingly regulated. In a parallel, but unrelated development, urban design has come of age as an independent discipline.

Accessible introductions to twentieth-century Dutch urbanism are scarce enough in Dutch, let alone in English. Since the publication in the 1960s of R. Blijstra's Nederlandse stedenbouw na 1900 (Town-planning in the Netherlands since 1900) **the only other book of this kind has been** Ruimtelijke Ordening **by H. van der Cammen and L.A. de Klerk. This successful 1986 publication (revised edition 1993) devotes extensive attention to urban design from the broader perspective of spatial planning. Both these publications have served me as models in putting together the current book:** Ruimtelijke ordening **because of the clarity of the text and the quantity of information it conveys and Blijstra's book because of its superb illustrations.**

The publication of this book was made possible by the generous support of the Netherlands Architecture Fund. I would also like to take this opportunity to thank Maike Oosterbaan who assisted me with research and in the selection of illustrative material, Ingrid Oosterheerd for her work as picture editor and Caroline Gautier for the final editing. Finally, Lex Reitsma has produced a design to equal the one he did for 20th Century Architecture in the Netherlands**.**

Hans Ibelings, Amsterdam, November 1999

20th Century Urban Design in the Netherlands

Contents

1900-1910

City building

The Netherlands at the turn of the century was a country of villages and small towns. Out of a total population of over five million, half lived in communities of fewer than five thousand inhabitants. In 1900 there were only 24 municipalities with more than 20,000 inhabitants and even the three largest cities, Amsterdam, Rotterdam and The Hague, were still relatively small by world standards despite a period of rapid growth at the end of the nineteenth century. Smallness of scale also characterized the Dutch landscape.

Compared with other countries, urbanization got off to a late start in the Netherlands. It was not until the end of the nineteenth century that migration from the countryside to the cities, in combination with a substantial population increase, led to rapid urban growth. Here as elsewhere, one of the major forces powering urbanization was the shift in employment from agriculture to trade, services and, above all, industry. Although not confined to urban areas, industrial activity did tend to concentrate in and around towns and cities. Apart from the big cities in the west of the country industrialization also left its mark on places like Zaandam, Tilburg, Eindhoven, Enschede, Hengelo and the towns and villages of the Limburg mining region. In addition to factories, warehouses, silos and the like, housing estates were built to accommodate the industrial labourers.

Paralleling this sudden upsurge in urbanization, was a much smaller movement of (affluent) people in the opposite direction. One of the main reasons for this minor exodus from the cities was described thus by the architect H. van der Kloot Meijburg in 1906: 'As the big cities have spread and in so doing sacrificed much of their appeal to the demands of modern life, so the tide of those who have moved hearth and home to places where the nerve-racking urban bustle has not yet penetrated has grown.' These ex-urban hearths were located in 'villa parks', the upmarket residential areas that were starting to shoot up in the woods and dunes outside the towns, usually as a result of private initiative. They transformed the natural landscape into picturesque parks in accordance with the principles of the English landscape style, with winding roads, apparently random greenery and asymmetrical water features.

The same landscaping techniques, incidentally, were applied to upper-class housing developments in urban areas. A similar park-like layout dominated much of H.P. Berlage's first extension plan for Amsterdam South, for example. Drawn up between 1900 and 1905, the plan's spacious layout allowed for too few houses to be financially viable and it was never executed.

Extension plans of the size of Berlage's Amsterdam South were not unknown in the nineteenth century, but at the beginning of the twentieth century they became mandatory for municipalities with more than ten thousand inhabitants or a population increase of over twenty per cent during the previous five years. In fact this statutory obligation, incorporated in the Housing Act of 1901, applied only to the indication of roads, water mains and buildings. Municipalities were not required to go into detail about land use. When the province of Gelderland requested the city of Arnhem to lay down specific land allocations in its extension plan of 1904, the city council demurred — citing the Housing Act — on the grounds that any additional regulation would restrict the freedom of private developers who might then decide to abandon their development plans altogether. Not every municipality attached such importance to private interest, however, for in many places the plans drawn up were a great deal more detailed than required by law.

7   Such a wealth of detail is typical of an approach that dominated town planning practice from the late nineteenth century into 1920s: city building. Its main premise was that the 'utility issue' as H.P. Berlage called it, should be handled in an aesthetically sensitive manner. This aesthetic cityscape was pursued by means of a coherent spatial composition of streets, squares and public gardens. The principal element in this type of urban design plan is the architecture and in particular housing: the continuous facades of large housing and building blocks define the nature of the urban space they enclose. Thanks to the Housing Act, which provided for favourable loans from local and central government, it became financially feasible to build such large blocks, at least in the big cities. In many small municipalities Housing Act loans were used to build more modest projects varying from a few houses to a complete neighbourhood. Initially, housing construction in the big cities had also consisted chiefly of small projects but the Housing Act gave housing associations so much financial scope that they were able to contemplate building whole street frontages and entire city blocks. Production was slow to get going, however, and several city councils decided to go ahead and build their own housing complexes in order to tackle the housing shortage that was at its most acute in the overcrowded slum areas. The Housing Act forbade such conditions but its chief weapon, the condemnation order, proved fairly ineffectual. In many cases private property owners lacked the means or the will to carry out the necessary improvements and so in practice very little changed, not least because there was no alternative accommodation available for those who lost their dwelling in this way. Nonetheless, in the long term the act did lead to the eradication of the worst slums and unhealthiest conditions.

The concern for public health expressed in the Housing Act exemplifies a perception of the city as an unwholesome place, an idea that was to crop up again and again in the ensuing decades. The Act duly provided for hygienic measures designed to improve conditions. Apart from the slum areas, the main target of such measures was the intermixing of houses and factories, a practice also perceived as unhealthy. Many urban development plans of the time reflect this ambition to separate housing and industry but it was not until well into the twentieth century that such separation became a reality.

It was seen as the town planner's task to resolve such practical issues in an aesthetically pleasing manner in a large, coherent composition: to turn urban planning into the art of building cities. At the beginning of the century it was possible to distinguish two main schools of thought in city building, a formal and an informal, characterized by Berlage as the stylized and the picturesque. In the first, the emphasis was on symmetry and axes. Cities from the Baroque period were usually regarded as representing the apogee of this formal approach. In the second, the emphasis was on a harmony of irregular organization, as exemplified by the mediaeval city. Berlage himself preferred the Baroque model, as his plan for The Hague makes clear. Interestingly, this plan incorporated the design K.P.C. de Bazel had made for a World Capital, an idealistic initiative of the Norwegian-American sculptor H.C. Andersen. The perfect regularity of the star-shaped layout reflects the ideal nature of this city which was to be the seat of institutions dedicated to international interests, world peace and progress.

Both versions of city building proceeded on the basis of a clear hierarchy in the city, a hierarchy that is visible at the two-dimensional level in the distinction between centre and periphery and in the presence of clear cardinal directions in neighbourhoods and districts. In three dimensions the hierarchy is chiefly visible in the accentuation of key points by large and often tall buildings. Most of those engaged in town planning in the Netherlands were architects, which goes some way towards explaining the bias towards the architectural aspects of urbanism. Their other main point of reference was German professional literature where they encountered and absorbed the views of theorists of the likes of J. Stübben, K. Henrici, A.E. Brinckmann and above all C. Sitte. These views were sufficiently well-known among Dutch town planners for one of the entrants in the Amsterdam Dam Square Competition of 1908 to give his plan the motto 'Camillo Sitte'. Entrants in this competition were asked to produce 'a general development plan and an aesthetic townscape for Dam Square and environs that satisfies the requirements of traffic and amenity while also taking account of financial feasibility. Participation in this competition is open to all Dutch nationals'. As the last phrase indicates, town planning was not yet seen as the exclusive preserve of any particular professional group. In the event, all the premiated competition entries were by architects, among whom were the partners Van Gendt and E. Cuypers. The competition was won by the Amsterdam School architect J. van der Mey but his design was never implemented, an outcome that is even more common in urban planning than in architecture.

The competition for Dam Square was one of many design contests held for inner urban areas in the first decades of the twentieth century. This is hardly surprising for it was precisely these areas where the effects of an increase in scale, uni-functional development and heavier traffic – a trio of problems that continued to plague planners throughout the century – were making themselves felt. The process began with the construction of large office buildings on numerous sites in many city centres around the country. The businesses, banks and insurance companies who built these imposing edifices were responding to a growing demand for office space sparked off by the economic revival that had begun around 1895. Because of the interdependent nature of these businesses and the major role played by mutual contacts, it was both practical and necessary to settle in close proximity to one another. This initial concentration of commerce and services in turn encouraged the establishment of cafés, restaurants, hotels, shops and department stores, a process that gradually ousted housing from the centre of the city. The next step, aimed at providing better accessibility to these centres of commerce, involved building new traffic corridors and widening main thoroughfares. In this way the close-grained fabric of many historic town centres was rudely disrupted by a new pattern with very different dimensions.

9   The pursuit of a form of aesthetic coherence continued to play a major role in town planning into the 1930s. And even after this, plans continued to be made in which the aesthetic ordering of the urban space, with clearly defined streets and squares, was of primary importance. Examples include the plan for the expansion of Amsterdam drawn up on their own initiative by A. Staal, A. Komter and Zanstra, Giesen & Sijmons during the Second World War, and various plans from the 1980s and 1990s, such as J. Coenen's masterplan for Vaillantlaan in The Hague. The longevity of ideas is typical of urban planning practice, as is their slowness to catch on in the first place. It often takes a long time for new concepts to be put into practice. For example, the Garden City idea was introduced – in England – around 1900. Although it struck an almost immediate chord with Dutch town planners it was not until the late 1910s that the first suburbs based on this concept were actually built in the Netherlands.

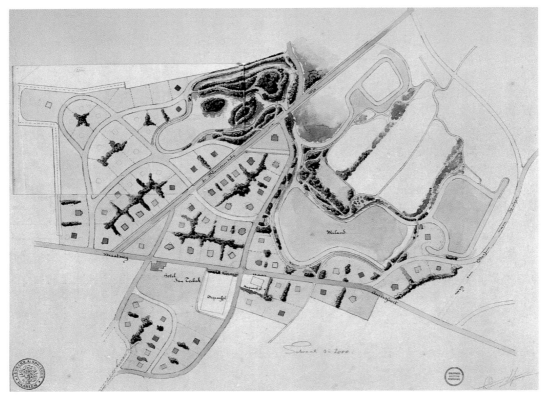

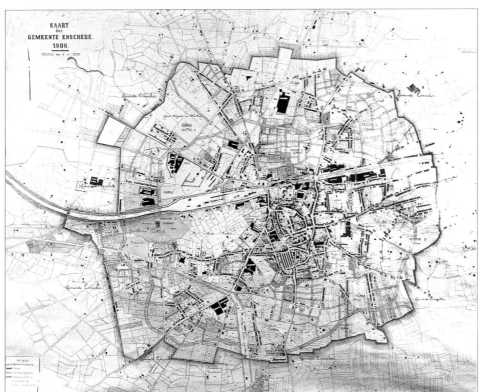

L. Springer villa park plan, Oud-Bussum (1903)

A.H. Op ten Noort general extension plan, Enschede (1906)

J.H. de Roos, W.S. Overeijnder   housing Mussenberg, Arnhem (1910)

housing Schilderswijk, The Hague (1908)

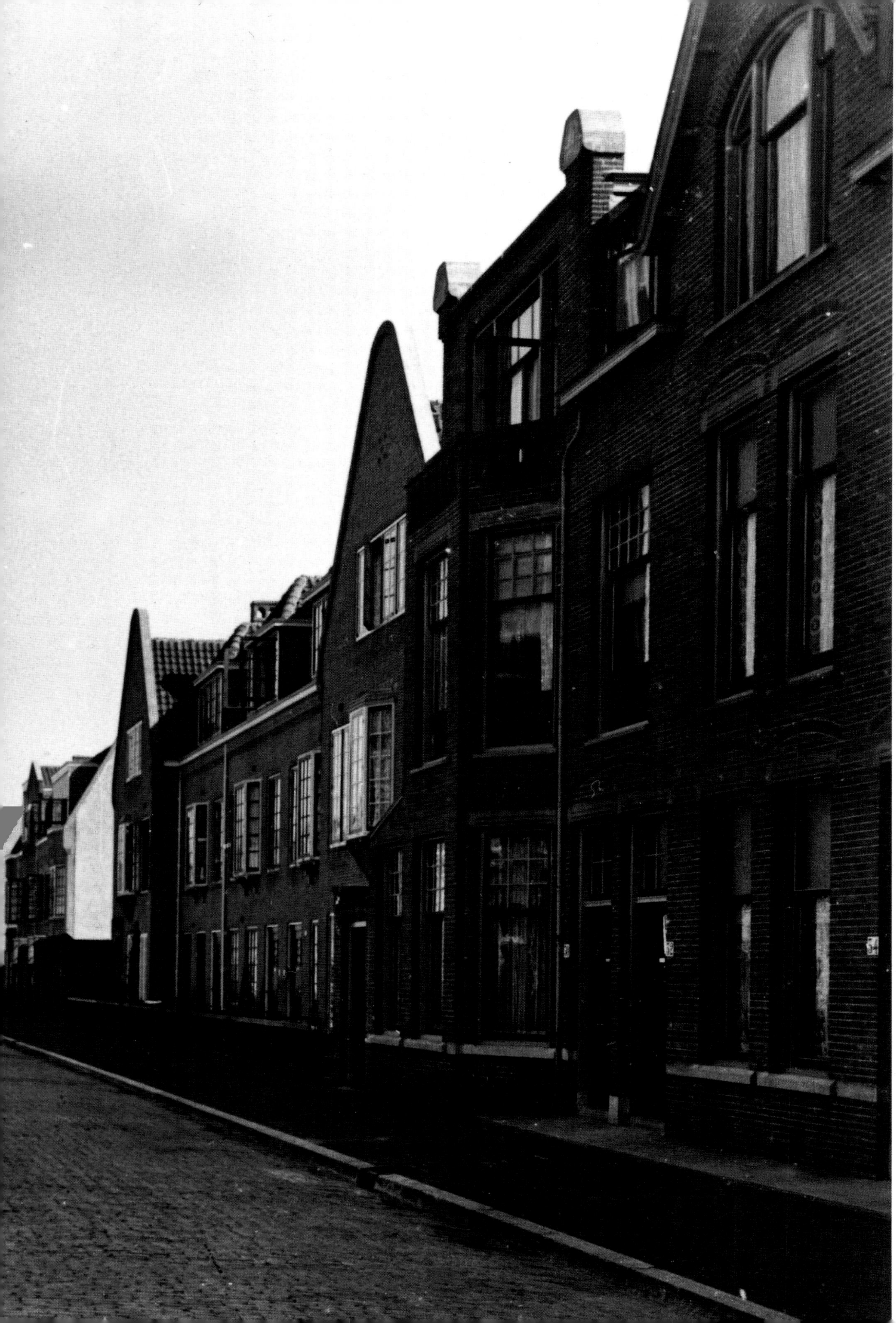

mansions Statenkwartier, The Hague (c. 1905)

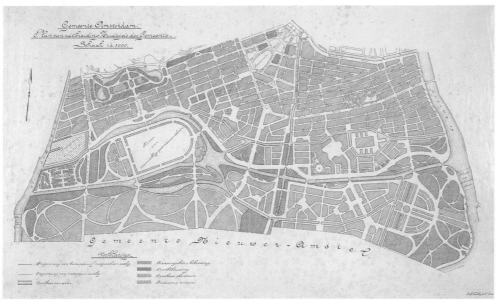

J.E. van der Pek   housing, Amsterdam-West (1909)

H.P. Berlage   first extension plan Amsterdam-South (1900-1905)

J.E. van der Pek housing Frederik Hendrikstraat, Amsterdam (1909)

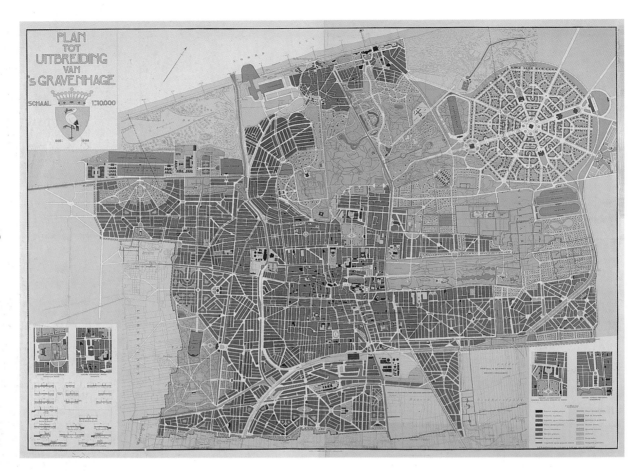

H.P. Berlage extension plan, The Hague (1907-1911)

H.P. Berlage perspective study for square in extension plan, The Hague (1907-1911)

17

J.F. Staal, A.J. Kropholler Utrecht office building, Amsterdam (1904-1906)

18

F.J. Nieuwenhuis   extension plan, Utrecht (1910)

Nachtegaalstraat during the widening operation, Utrecht (1910)

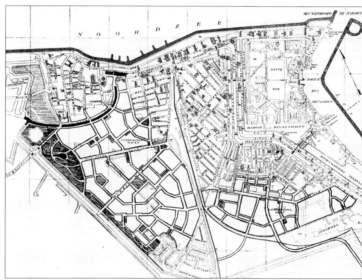

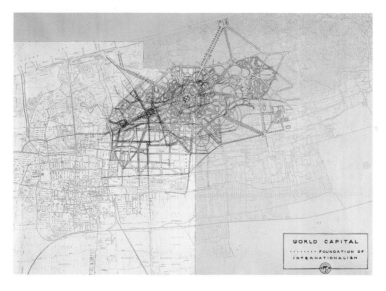

extension plan, Groningen (1906-1907)

W. van Boven   extension plan, Den Helder (1909)

K.P.C. de Bazel   design for a World Capital (1905)

1910-1920

Garden city and city block

One of the most potent influences on Dutch town planning during the 1910s was the garden city concept. The theoretical guideline was contained in the ideas of the Englishman E. Howard; practical models were available in the form of actual garden cities, garden villages and garden suburbs, chiefly in England and Germany. Howard had introduced his garden city ideal in 1898 in To-Morrow: A Peaceful Path to Real Reform, a book that was republished in 1902 as Garden Cities of To-Morrow. In response to the over-crowding and uncontrolled growth of cities Howard had developed the concept of a concentrically arranged new town with no more than thirty thousand inhabitants and containing all the amenities required for self-sufficiency. The civic centre at the heart of the plan was surrounded by a ring of green and spacious residential areas which in turn was ringed by a belt of parkland that acted as a buffer between the housing and the outermost, industrial ring. A further band of agricultural land outside the city boundaries completed the picture. The concentric layout gave the town a self-contained form and precluded further expansion.

While no genuine garden city was ever built in the Netherlands, Howard's notion of an 'Arcadian' urbanity was warmly embraced. Village-like housing estates sprang up all over the place as an alternative to the stone city. But apart from their abundant greenery and village atmosphere, these estates scarcely lived up to Howard's description of the garden city. They were not complete towns but mere suburbs, they were located not outside but inside or adjacent to the city, and they were not concentrically laid out.

The leafy village look was also to be found in the workers' housing estates some factory managers had built for their workforce. Apart from a few early examples such as Agnetapark in Delft (1883) designed by the landscape architect L.P. Zocher, the majority of such industrial villages date from the 1910s. This was the period when Philips in Eindhoven commissioned K.P.C. de Bazel, W. Hanrath and J.G.J. de Jongh to build the Philips Village, J. Rothuizen built Heveadorp in Renkum for workers at the Hevea rubber factory, H.A.J. Baanders designed Heyplaat for employees of the Rotterdam Droogdokmaatschappij and in Utrecht Elinkwijk was built for railway construction workers employed by Werkspoor. Elinkwijk was designed by K. Muller who also built 't Lansink in Hengelo for the Stork company. 't Lansink differs from other company towns not only because of its architectural and urbanistic qualities, but also because it was not exclusively reserved for Stork employees.

Industrial villages can no doubt be criticized for reinforcing the inequitable balance of power between workers and management by extending the latter's control over employees outside working hours. Even the rusticity of such villages was illusory, built as they were in the shadow of factory chimneys, but this does not alter the fact that they usually provided workers with a better living environment than they would have been able to afford elsewhere.

How to reconcile the rural tranquillity of the garden city with the harsh reality of modern urban life was a problem that preoccupied M.J. Granpré Molière. In the 1910s he was one of the designers of Vreewijk, a large residential development in south Rotterdam. In 1921 he wrote that though it might be going too far to call the garden city an 'organized flight from society' there was certainly 'a tendency in that direction'. Granpré Molière saw the garden village as a typical sign of the times and as only one possibility. He claimed that in addition to 'garden city construction' there was also 'monumental town house construction'. Neither of these options was 'in itself the solution' but both could be justified in a modern age that was characterized by 'the combination of everything seemingly contradictory'. Since in his view 'housing and urban design [were] a faithful reflection of social life', it seemed only logical to him that the two tendencies should co-exist.

'Garden city construction' appeared all over the Netherlands, in big and small municipalities alike. 'Monumental town house construction' on the other hand was confined to the big cities, in particular Amsterdam and Rotterdam, where it made its appearance in the course of the 1910s. The big housing schemes by J.E. van der Pek, H.P. Berlage, H.J.M. Walenkamp, K.P.C. de Bazel and M. de Klerk in Amsterdam and by M. Brinkman and J.J.P. Oud in Rotterdam display a wide range of approaches to this new building task.

Walenkamp's Zaanhof in Amsterdam can be seen as a traditional courtyard building, only on a very large scale. The inner ring of buildings focused on the court is encircled by a second, outer-directed ring designed by Ingwersen and Kuipers, a configuration that gives Zaanhof two faces, an outer, urban face and an inner, village-like inner face. A similar approach informs Brinkman's superblock in Spangen (Rotterdam), although here the court contains housing after the fashion of the big housing schemes in Berlin. One curiosity of this inner-directed Spangen project is the gallery at second-floor level which is so wide that it functions as a raised internal street.

Such inward-looking complexes are the exception rather than the rule among the large housing blocks. Most of the housing schemes built in the 1910s consist of perimeter blocks where the dwellings are oriented towards the street. The inner courts did, however, often contain buildings. Oud's blocks in Spangen contain school buildings while in De Klerk's housing block on Spaarndammer-plantsoen in Amsterdam there is a building for the residents' association. De Klerk's block stands out among all these other perimeter blocks by virtue of its elevational variety. Most housing complexes are characterized by an austere regularity in which the individual dwelling is lost in the larger whole.

The city composed of superblocks is nowhere more strikingly manifested than in Berlage's second plan for Amsterdam South (1915-1917). Plan Zuid, as it came to be known, owed its existence to a clause in the Housing Act obliging municipalities to revise their extension plans after ten years. Although the first plan of 1904 had failed to qualify for implementation, it was a legally recognized extension plan under the terms of the act and therefore had to be revised. In the event, Berlage was invited to draw up this second plan too. This design turned out be both more realistic and more radical with respect to building density. The radicality relates chiefly to the consistency with which dwellings are expressed as mass-produced units that merge to form large housing blocks. In Plan Zuid the housing block becomes the measure of things. Berlage's second plan is exceptionally large and generously dimensioned: the streets are wide, the parks and green spaces spaciously laid out and the housing blocks massive. Although construction began in the 1920s, it was not until just before the Second World War that this high point of Dutch urban planning was finally completed.

Large-scale development was not confined to housing schemes in the new expansion areas, however. This period also saw the construction of many of

the big buildings around Dam Square in Amsterdam, including the Bijenkorf department store and the Industria office building, while in Rotterdam the city fathers were busy turning the Coolsingel into a monumental boulevard with the town hall by H. Evers and the central post office building by C.G. Bremer as major landmarks. This boulevard was intended to signal that Rotterdam, with its burgeoning population and thriving harbour, was now a full-fledged metropolis.

The growth in population, the increase in traffic and the expansion of industry and commerce led everywhere to greater pressure on space. The question of who should steer this development in the right direction has been a frequent subject of debate during the twentieth century. One such debate was conducted in 1913 and 1914 in the pages of the Bouwkundig Weekblad. It was triggered off by an article by J.H.E. Rückert published in the engineering periodical De Ingenieur. Appointed Director of Public Works in Tilburg in 1913, Rückert was in charge of overseeing the implementation of Tilburg's General Extension Plan of 1917. He expressed the view that urban planning was the territory of the 'aesthetically and architecturally informed engineer', by which he meant his own professional group of military and civil engineers. The only task for architects as he saw it was to provide an aesthetic envelope for the solution those engineers came up with to the utilitarian issue. The Bouwkundig Weekblad, as was to be expected from a journal for architects, argued passionately in favour of a leading role for the architect in urban planning projects. One of the arguments it advanced was that 'architecture is not confined to the building and its internal arrangements, but also encompasses the massing of buildings. This massing gives shape to streets and squares which, together with the buildings, make up the constituent parts of the city'. This laconic summary by W.F.C. Schaap of the prevailing city-building view that buildings make the city, can be seen as an attempt to substantiate the claim that urban planning was part of architecture. Not everyone agreed, however. In 1913, for example, the architecture department of Delft Technical College failed in its bid to have a professor of urban design appointed. The parliament, with whom the decision rested, did not consider such a chair necessary and so official recognition of urban planning as an independent discipline was temporarily shelved. Nonetheless, after the 1910s a process of professionalization began to make itself felt. It was prompted by, among other things, the foundation of the Nederlandsch Instituut voor Volkshuisvesting in 1918 (restyled three years later to include town planning as well as housing in its title), the international conferences on town planning held from the late 1910s onwards, the setting-up of separate municipal town planning departments and the emergence of architectural practices specializing in urban design projects, such as Granpré Molière and Verhagen & Kok. Another factor contributing to the professionalization of the discipline was its increasingly scientific basis whereby statistical data and demographic, traffic and economic forecasts provided the departure point for designs. As such, those who had argued that the utilitarian issue was the essence of the urban planning task and who appeared to come off worst in the Bouwkundig Weekblad debate, were eventually proved right.

23

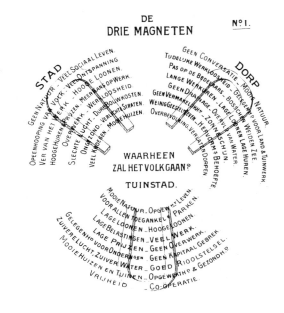

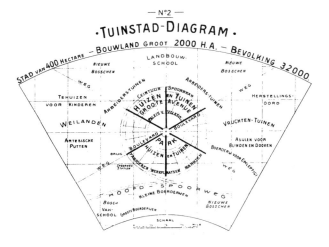

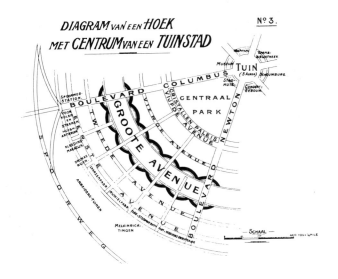

24

Dutch version of E. Howard's garden city diagrams

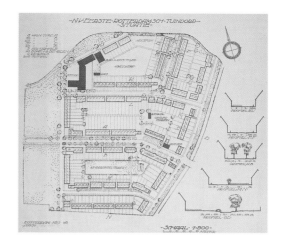

J. Rothuizen Hevea Village near Doornwerth (1916-1918)

M.J. Granpré Molière in collaboration with **P. Verhagen, J.H. de Roos, W.S. Overeijnder** Vreewijk

garden suburb, Rotterdam (1916-1919)

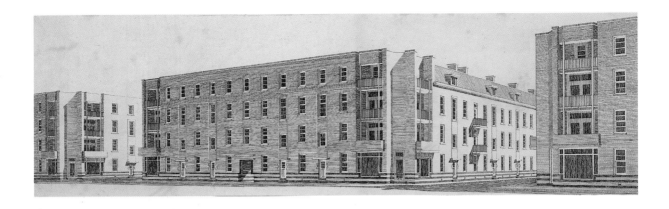

26

J.J.P. Oud housing Tusschendijken, Rotterdam (1919-1920, destroyed 1943)

M. de Klerk housing Spaarndammerbuurt, Amsterdam (1914-1925)

H.J.M. Walenkamp housing Spaarndammerbuurt, Amsterdam (1919)

K.P.C. de Bazel housing Spaarndammerbuurt, Amsterdam (1916)

H.P. Berlage extension plan, Amsterdam South (1915-1917)

H.P. Berlage extension plan in bird's-eye view, Amsterdam South (1915-1917)

B.T. Boeyinga, J.H. Mulder Oostzaan garden suburb, Amsterdam (1922-1924)

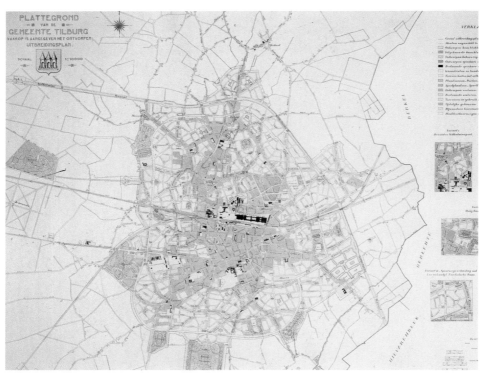

W.K. de Wijs, A.H. Op ten Noort Pathmos housing scheme, Enschede (1914-1928)

J.H.E. Rückert extension plan, Tilburg (1917)

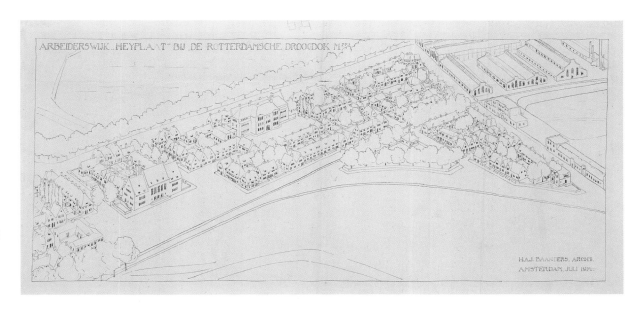

31

H.A.J. Baanders   Heyplaat garden suburb, Rotterdam (1915)

P.J. Hamers   Zuilen garden suburb, Utrecht (1915-1917)

32

J.B. Kam entrance Philips Village, Eindhoven (1915)

K.P.C. de Bazel, W. Hanrath, J.G.J. de Jongh   workers' housing complex in Philips Village,

Eindhoven (1910-1917)

J. Wils Daal en Berg Papaverhof housing scheme, The Hague (1919-1922)

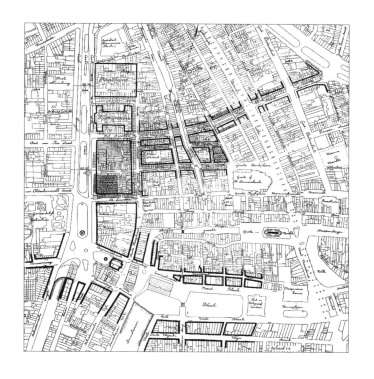

35

projected inner-city corridors, Rotterdam (1913)

Coolsingel, Rotterdam in the 1920s

M. Brinkman housing Spangen, Rotterdam (1919-1922)

K. Muller Het Lansink garden suburb, Hengelo (1911)

1920-1930

The regional city

City-building ideas and the garden city concept continued to dominate urban planning practice until well into the 1920s. Little by little, however, new ideas about architectural expression and urban design began to emerge. The physical implications of these new approaches can be seen most clearly in a few plans where the city of perimeter blocks made way for a city of free-standing housing blocks, terrace houses and high-rise apartment and office buildings surrounded by open space. These plans resulted in a cityscape that was fundamentally

different from the one produced by all those earlier designs in which streets and squares were enclosed by unbroken facades. For the time being, however, such plans were confined to the drawing-board. Changes in the way planners approached urban design assignments were gradual. Whereas it had previously been customary to spell out many if not all aspects in detail in the masterplan, this style of planning progressively gave way to an approach that was more concerned with the broad picture. This new approach allowed more scope for the changes and additions that often proved necessary or desirable during the course of what was usually a very long period of implementation. Such changes, for example, occurred in H.P. Berlage's second Plan Zuid. The Zuider railway station was never built and the projected August Allebéplein turned out very differently from the way Berlage had imagined it in the 1910s with the result that the main north-south axis through the district, Minervalaan, turned out to be much more residential in character than originally intended.

At the same time, planners were also starting to widen their horizons and to see urban issues in a regional context. The regional development of cities was discussed at length during the International Garden City and Town Planning Association conference held in Amsterdam in 1924. For Dutch town planners this conference marked the beginning of a tradition of regional planning. Thereafter they became increasingly accustomed to drawing up urban development plans whose effect did not stop at municipal boundaries.

The two most important examples of regional planning in the 1920s were W.G. Witteveen's 1928 plan for Rotterdam and the regional plan that J.M. de Casseres produced for Eindhoven in 1930. Witteveen and De Casseres (who had recently coined the word 'planology' to designate planning on a scale larger than that of the city) were convinced that it was impossible to steer urban growth in the right direction by means of separate local plans or even plans for an entire city. They felt that the city should be seen in a wider context and their plans reflect this attitude. Both men produced plans for an area that extended well beyond municipal boundaries. In Rotterdam the harbour and industry had expanded so much during the 1920s that the actual built-up area was larger than the city. In Eindhoven, where the annexation of neighbouring villages had boosted the size of the city, the main engine driving urban growth was the Philips company.

Witteveen's General Extension Plan, which provided for the annexation of several smaller communities in the surrounding area, was approved by the Rotterdam city council but not by the national government so it was never put into effect. Implementation would in any case have been hampered by the economic crisis that broke out shortly afterwards. Nonetheless, Witteveen continued to think in terms of a Greater Rotterdam when drawing up various local plans for the city. He treated them not as autonomous plans but as part of a larger whole, thus leaving open the option of regional planning at some later date. In De Casseres's case, the design for Eindhoven formed the prelude to the regional plans of the 1930s, much more comprehensive plans for large areas in which the 'survey', a preliminary economic and sociological study, played a vital role. English town planning was the main model in the field of regional development, hence the widespread use of the English term.

In the plans of both Witteveen and De Casseres much emphasis was placed on the highway network. Regulating traffic had always been a major element in urban development plans but now the issue of traffic in cities was tackled on a larger scale than ever before. Improvements to the infrastructure at city and regional level were aimed at optimizing connections and managing the ever-increasing flow of traffic. To give some idea of the magnitude of these traffic flows: the number of private cars multiplied sixfold between 1920 and 1930, albeit from a trifling figure of eleven thousand to a still modest seventy thousand. The preferred solutions to the urban traffic problem were the construction of one or more orbital roads, a system of radial roads or a combination of both. For the radial system it was often possible to widen and extend existing main streets and roads, while in the older towns the space occupied by ramparts or encircling canals often provided planners with a minimally disruptive route for an orbital road. On top of this, traffic was for the first time scrutinized at a national level. In 1927 the Ministry of Public Works published the first National Highways Plan, later followed in the 1930s by a comparable plan for the National Motorways.

Apart from looking for solutions to traffic problems, urban planners also directed their attention in these years to the separation of functions, in particular those of living and working. In many instances green space was a useful tool for achieving such separation. As with traffic, there were two models: a radial and a concentric model which were sometimes used in combination. In the radial model green space took the form of green triangles cutting into the city like wedges of cake. The concentric model was based on a stringing together of parks, green space and former town ramparts to form a continuous green belt around the city.

One of the instruments planners were able to wield in order to prevent unwanted mixed use was the zoning plan included in the revised Housing Act of 1921. Compared with the very summary demands placed on extension plans by the original act, the zoning plan imposed a much stricter framework. In reality the amendment simply confirmed what was already standard practice in many municipalities where extension plans determined not just the position of water mains, roads and buildings but also dictated land use.

While land allocation was being more precisely laid down in urban development plans, the growing interest in planning at a regional and even national level inevitably led to a greater degree of abstraction in town planning. Outline plans and 'main-point' plans became the order of the day, a development that culminated in the 1970s in a triumph of incompleteness known as the vlekken-plan. This emphasis on broad outlines has continued to dominate spatial planning for the greater part of the twentieth century.

One consequence of the increasing abstraction is that the basic urban design structure is often impossible to discern in what at first glace appears to be a mishmash of development. This 'invisibility' is usually reinforced by the fact that a particular area often bears traces of several plans that have been wholly or partially executed, one after the other. Only in those places where designs have been realized in full and in one go and with a more or less homogeneous architecture, is it still possible to detect the underlying structure. But where various hands have tinkered with an existing urban area, the result is a miscellany of ideas and concepts.

Throughout the 1920s the majority of urban design plans continued to be based on concepts developed in the previous century. Indeed, housing estates rooted in the tradition of the garden city concept – such as Nieuwendam in Amsterdam North – were still being built well into the 1930s. And architects like H.P. Berlage continued to interpret urban planning as urban architecture. Berlage designed Mercatorplein in Amsterdam, Hofplein in Rotterdam and produced – together with L.N. Holsboer – an extension plan for Utrecht in 1924. The last design, along the same lines as his Plan Zuid, was in one respect very much of its time in that it assigned a leading role to traffic. W.M. Dudok, the Hilversum city architect, also adhered to what were by then traditional urban design principles similar to those of Berlage. The extension plans he drew up for the town during the 1920s were designed to give Hilversum a self-contained form and a recognizable silhouette, thus creating a clear distinction between the built-up area and nature. He wanted to prevent Hilversum from spreading unchecked into the surrounding countryside. When it came to town planning, Dudok had a strong aesthetic bias. He saw it as his task to devise efficient and aesthetic solutions for the urban planning assignment and he attached great importance to the sculptural quality of the buildings. Dudok incidentally played down his planning activities in the overgrown village of Hilversum: 'Compared with the big urban development issues, village planning is mere chamber music.' Although he added that 'even chamber music may be orchestrally conceived'.

The truly new forms developed during the 1920s remained ideas on paper. The most important of these was undoubtedly the principle of open row housing as an alternative to the previously closed subdivisions. Tested for the first time in the 1930s, it would go on to become the universal starting-point for countless post-war urban design plans. The same period saw the first serious experiments with high-rise as an architectural and urban design tool. So far high-rise had been used sporadically and chiefly as an urban accent. Now there were proposals for housing schemes consisting entirely of high-rise buildings. H.T. Wijdeveld produced a design for residential tower blocks in a parkland setting, a plan he may have deliberately antedated to make it look as though it had preceded the now famous urban designs by Le Corbusier. In 1930 J. Duiker published Hoogbouw, a study of the possibilities for the widespread deployment of high-rise.

J.B. van Loghem   Tuinwijk-Zuid housing scheme, Haarlem (1919-1922)

H.T. Wijdeveld   Hoofdweg housing complex, Amsterdam (1923-1926)

W.G. Witteveen Dijkzigt/Land van Hoboken extension plan, Rotterdam (1926)

44

OTTO : SIMULTANÉITÉ

C. van Eesteren   competition design for shopping arcade with café, The Hague (1924)

W.M. Dudok revised extension plan, Hilversum (1927-1935)

W.M. Dudok housing, Hilversum

45

46

H.P. Berlage extension plan Groningen (1927-1928)

J.F. Staal Victorieplein high-rise, Amsterdam South (1927-1930)

47

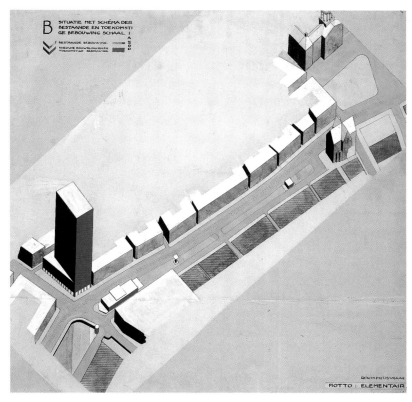

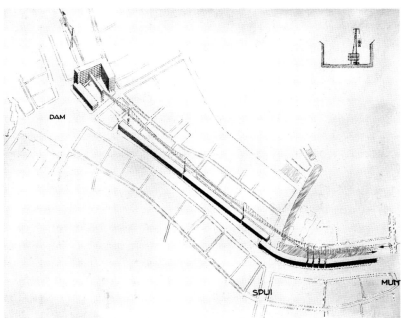

C. van Eesteren   competition design for reorganization of Rokin, Amsterdam (1924-1926)

M. Stam   competition design for reorganization of Rokin, Amsterdam (1924-1926)

H.P. Berlage   plan for Hofplein, Rotterdam (1926)

M. Stam plan for Hofplein, Rotterdam (1926)

50

J. Duiker, J.G. Wiebenga   design for high-rise (1927-1930)

H.P. Berlage   Mercatorplein, Amsterdam (1924-1927)

51

H.T. Wijdeveld   design for a national park between Amsterdam and Zandvoort (1926-1927)

1930-1940

The functional city

It had become clear during the 1920s that many urban planning issues extended beyond municipal boundaries and consequently called for a regional approach. This obviously applied to big cities like Rotterdam and Eindhoven, but even in smaller towns and villages there were many spatial issues that were better dealt with in a regional perspective. In 1931 regional planning was given official legal status in a new amendment to the Housing Act. Henceforth municipalities were empowered to set up joint committees to draw up a regional plan. The reasoning behind the amendment was that a joint plan would enable municipalities to resolve clashes of interest and to take better account of large-scale effects such as population growth, migration, increases in traffic and the size and location of industry at regional level.

The rise of regional planning resulted in greater prominence for research. Before any plan could be made it was first necessary to collect detailed information about a region's current demographic and economic situation and to then use this information to forecast future developments. On the basis of such a survey a regional plan could then be devised. This logical course of events was in practice frequently frustrated by the difficulty of gathering the required data. Reliable forecasts of, say, trends in population growth, prosperity and traffic density were often hampered by the lack of sound statistical research.

Partly because of this, regional planning delivered few tangible results in the 1930s. The plans that did get made, got no further than the drawing-board. Despite this, practitioners were already thinking about the following stage. This further widening of horizons to encompass the entire country was not only dictated by logic but also reflected urban designers' growing awareness of the need to master all levels of spatial planning. That large-scale spatial planning was a discipline in its own right was underscored by the foundation in 1935 of the Association of Dutch Urban Designers (BNS), the counterpart of the Association of Dutch Architects (BNA). The idea of national planning was first mooted in the early 1920s, after which it was fleshed out in the course of the 1930s by J.M. de Casseres. Finally, in 1939, W.B. Kloos published a book entitled Het Nationaal Plan. In his introduction, Kloos described the National Plan as a step on the way to a 'European Plan': 'The only means of approaching the highest ideal, of ensuring the greatest possible integrity of the whole is via international cooperation in which the national presence of each individual country fits harmoniously into the international overall picture.' Kloos himself considered such an idealistic cooperation impossible 'under present political conditions'. The Second World War did not, however, halt the trend towards national planning. On the day that the German army invaded the Netherlands a committee appointed to look into the setting up of a National Plan published its report. During the German occupation (1940-1945) their proposals led to the establishment of the Government Agency for the National Plan, the fore-runner of today's National Spatial Planning Agency.

Although the regional plans drawn up at this time seldom resulted in concrete steps, the regional approach to spatial issues did yield various new insights. One of these was that the western part of the Netherlands was one great urban-ized area. Flying over the province of South Holland in 1938, the aviation pion-eer A. Plesman noticed what T.K. van Lohuizen had already observed a decade earlier in his study The Holland-Utrecht urban sphere of influence, namely, that the four big cities (Amsterdam, The Hague, Rotterdam and Utrecht) of this region together formed a separate entity. Plesman dubbed this incipient con-urbation the Randstad (literally 'rim-city'), a name that has stuck. Not all the new insights were as conceptual as this. Sometimes they were very practical as can be seen in the draft design for Streekplan Oost-Utrecht (regional plan for East Utrecht) by Granpré Molière and Verhagen & Kok. Writing in the Tijd-schrift voor Volkshuisvesting en Stedebouw (Journal of housing and town plan-ning) in 1935, Van Lohuizen credited this 'first example of a Dutch regional plan' with a 'liberating significance'. It demonstrated that if development to the east of Utrecht were to proceed at the current rate, it would result in suffi-cient housing for an additional one million people by the year 2000, whereas the total population of the Netherlands was expected to rise by only five mil-lion by that date. On the basis of this calculation the designers consequently came to the conclusion that unbridled speculative housing construction should be curbed. The best way of achieving this was to designate a large part of the region as nature reserve. Nature and development were to be transected by a system of 'nature lanes', green zones four hundred metres wide on either side of the main motorways that would give motorists the impression of driving through a completely natural area. One way or another, a lot of green space was laid out in the cities during the 1930s. This was partly in response to the city dweller's demand for open-air recreation and partly as a means of giving work to the unemployed in a period of economic crisis. During the depression years Amsterdam, The Hague and Rotterdam all acquired public parks and woods by way of job-creation projects. In The Hague Zuiderpark was completed in this way and in Rotterdam the Kralingse Bos, the first designs for which had been made in the 1920s by M.J. Granpré Molière and J. Klijnen, was laid out according to a revised plan by Witteveen. In Amsterdam the Amsterdamse Bos was planted. The design for this extensive public park was made by J. Mulder, an employee of the Amsterdam Public Works Department.

The Amsterdamse Bos was part of the Amsterdam General Extension Plan (known by its Dutch initials, AUP) which acquired official status in 1934 and which has gone down in history as one of the most complete examples of func-tionalist town planning. The AUP contained countless elements of the 'func-tional city'. This was the title of a congress organized in 1933 by the CIAM

(Congrès Internationaux d'Architecture Moderne) and presided over by C. van Eesteren who, together with Van Lohuizen, was responsible for the Amsterdam AUP. Founded in 1928, CIAM was an alliance of individuals and associations committed to the idea of a modern architecture and urbanism. The opinions aired at CIAM's congresses on town planning did not differ greatly from the general consensus in urbanist circles at that time. What set the concept of the 'functional city' apart was its radical approach to generally accepted notions. The widely espoused spatial separation of functions, for example, acquired a very specific interpretation in the 'functional city' where urban life was reduced to four main functions (home, work, recreation and traffic) which were to be rigidly separated from one another spatially. In CIAM, the importance attached since the late nineteenth century to the hygienic component of town planning found expression in the slogan 'light, air and space'. Translated into planning practice this meant open development, with an adequate supply of fresh air and sunlight. In CIAM circles this was usually described as a 'rational method of development', a reference to the title of the 1930 congress. The best layout for achieving the desired penetration of light was one in which the rows of housing were placed slightly off a true north-south axis with the elevations facing almost due east and west. It was also important to place the rows of housing far enough apart so that they did not end up standing in one another's shadow during the winter months.

Elaborations of these principles appeared in various submissions for the Amsterdam competition for low-cost working class housing held in 1934. The plans in which row housing was used (which included those by G. Rietveld, W. van Tijen, J.H. van den Broek, the Bodon group, J.H. Groenewegen, C.J.F. Karsten and B. Merkelbach and A. Staal together with S. van Woerden and G.H. Holt) were all based on the same rationale of adequate sunlight. Van den Broek's plan was the odd man out in that it proposed a variation in building height. While the rows in nearly all the other plans were four storeys high, Van den Broek included a couple of twelve-storey flats in his plan. The competition was for a fictional location which made it relatively easy to achieve a rational method of development with a north-south subdivision. In none of the plans however was the principle of row housing so rigidly applied as to produce cross streets lined by blank end elevations. All the plans managed in some way or another to produce a more lively street frontage with shops, for example, and in some cases even dwellings, the 'unfavourable' orientation notwithstanding.

The entries for the competition for low-cost housing can be seen as part of a series of experiments with row subdivisions. Van Tijen built De Pol in Zutphen in 1932, J.J.P. Oud designed row housing for Blijdorp in Rotterdam and Merkelbach and Karsten did the same in the Amsterdam district of Bos en Lommer. In fact, building had already begun in Bos en Lommer when it was incorporated into the General Extension Plan. This explains why the district is something of a compromise in which the structure follows the original design but open row housing has been added in an attempt to achieve the desired 'rational development'. The most westerly part of Bos en Lommer, for which there was no prior plan, consists entirely of row housing, as does the neighbouring new suburb of Slotermeer, designed in 1939. Here the planners opted for an open subdivision, for the most part in rows running north to south. In propagating the term 'functional city' the functionalists created the impression that they had a monopoly on a logical and practical approach to urban design problems. This was not the case however. Planners who did not belong to the CIAM camp were every bit as convinced of the need for 'light, air and space'. Merkelbach acknowledged as much in 1932 in an article in De 8 en Opbouw in which he compared E. May's Römerstadt district in Frankfurt with Vreewijk in Rotterdam designed by Granpré Molière and Verhagen & Kok. In a footnote he praised Vreewijk for the 'correctness of its orientation, its unpretentiousness, its humanity and sensitivity', although he was less complimentary about what he saw as the 'childish play with corners and curves'. Granpré Molière came in for similar criticism for the villages he had designed in the new Wieringermeer Polder. Their romantic character was an eyesore as far as the functionalists were concerned. On the whole though functionalists and traditionalists tended to fight less over matters of town planning than of architecture. One point on which they did differ was the degree to which they were prepared to embrace open development as an urban planning principle. For this was not just about universally acceptable standards of light, air and space that everybody could agree were worth pursuing. It was also about an aesthetically motivated preference for an open and dynamic cityscape.

56

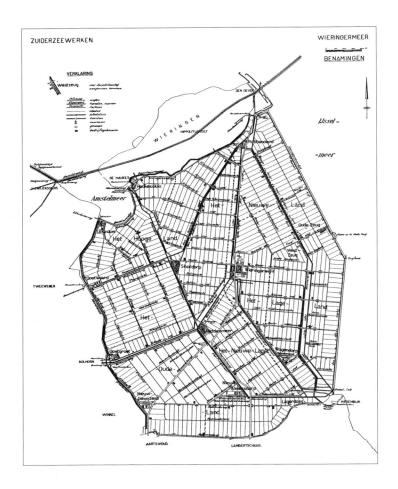

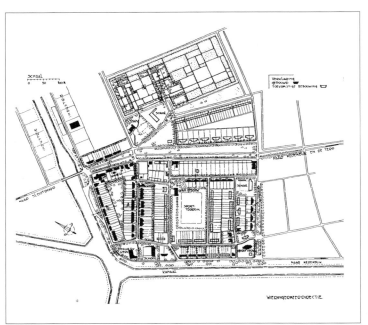

M.J. Granpré Molière, F. Ligtenberg sub-division plan Wieringermeerpolder (1929)

M.J. Granpré Molière urban design plan, Middenmeer (1931-1932)

M.J. Granpré Molière, J.F. Berghoef Middenmeer in the Wieringermeerpolder (1933-1941)

W.M. Dudok De Burgh garden suburb, Eindhoven (1937-1938)

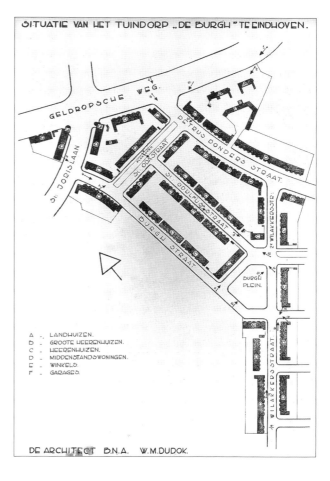

SITUATIE VAN HET TUINDORP „DE BURGH" TE EINDHOVEN.

A - . LANDHUIZEN.
B - . GROOTE HEERENHUIZEN.
C - . HEERENHUIZEN.
D - . MIDDENSTANDSWONINGEN.
E - . WINKELS.
F - . GARAGES.

DE ARCHITECT B.N.A. W.M.DUDOK.

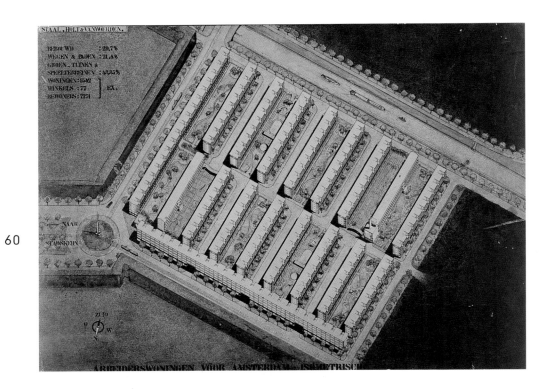

60

A. Staal, G.H. Holt, S. van Woerden   competition design Low-Cost Workers' Housing, motto & (1936)

J.H. van den Broek   competition design Low-Cost Workers' Housing, motto Optimum (1936)

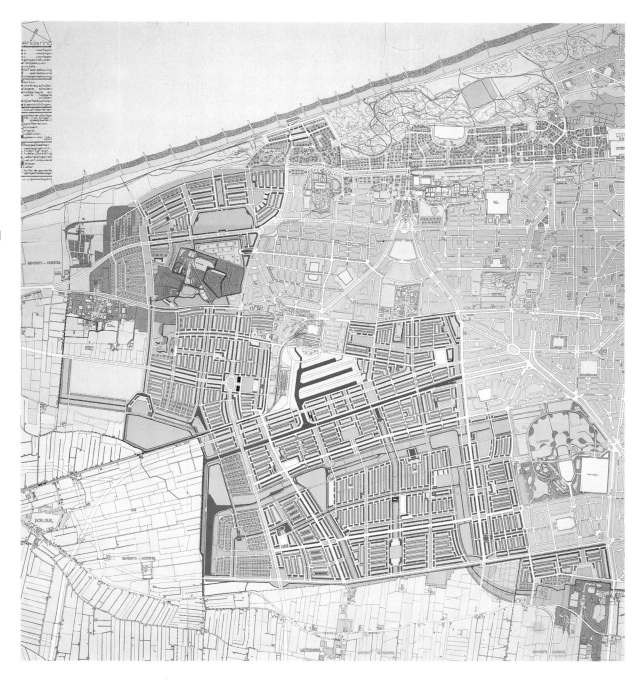

W.M. Dudok   extension plans Ockenburgh, Escamp- and Maepolder, Mariahoeve, Reigersbergen,

in The Hague (1934-1942)

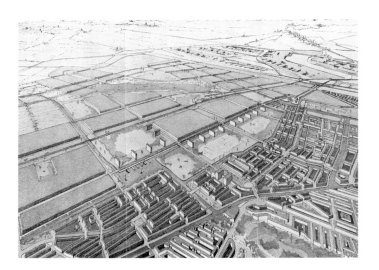

J. Mulder   masterplan Amsterdamse Bos, Amsterdam (1937)

C. van Eesteren   General Extension Plan, Amsterdam (1934)

C. van Eesteren   detail of General Extension Plan in bird's-eye view, Amsterdam (1934)

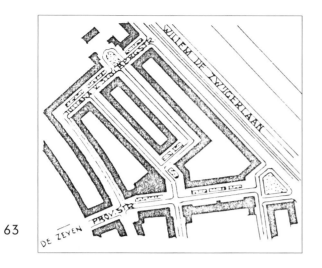

63

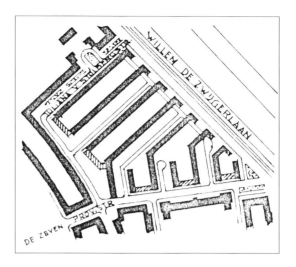

B. Merkelbach, C.J.F. Karsten   housing Bos en Lommer, Amsterdam (1935-1938)

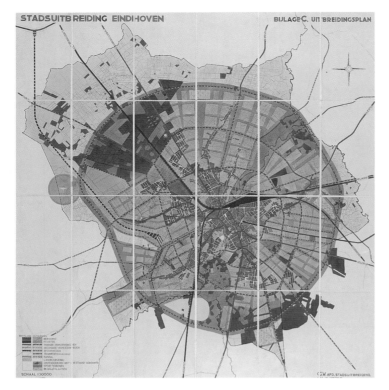

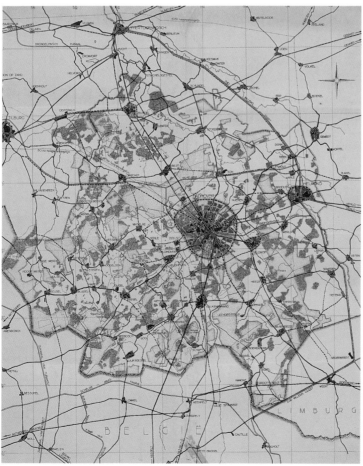

J.M. de Casseres   general extension plan, Eindhoven (1930)

J.M. de Casseres   regional plan south-east part of North Brabant (c. 1931)

64

J.J.P. Oud   design for housing Blijdorp, Rotterdam (1931)

1940-1950

Post-war reconstruction

The Second World War had far-reaching consequences for urban design and spatial planning in the Netherlands. The enormous physical damage inflicted during the five years of war severely dislocated many cities, towns and villages. On top of this, large sections of the infrastructure had been destroyed. Very little building was carried out during the German occupation and certainly nothing on a large scale. On the other hand, planning for post-war reconstruction had been in full swing since 1940, with urbanists and architects addressing themselves to the country's future and to the tasks they anticipated having to deal with when the war was over. Most of this planning was carried out within the existing and new official structures (under German command from May 1940), and to a lesser degree by people acting in a private capacity or in small groups. Plans for the reconstruction of Rotterdam and Middelburg, the two cities badly damaged in the first bombardments in 1940, were drawn up at the beginning of the war and in the case of Middelburg a start was even made on implementation. Reconstruction plans for towns and cities that were not damaged until 1944 or 1945 were drawn up shortly before the end of the war and immediately after liberation. Sometimes this was carried out with enormous energy and speed, as in Nijmegen which was severely damaged by allied bombing in 1944 and for which the broad outlines for reconstruction were mapped out in 1945. In other cities, such as Groningen, it took years before any decision was taken about the manner of reconstruction. Lack of political agreement was the main reason for such delays. Even where reconstruction plans were quick to materialize, the scale of the damage, the shortage of building materials and the desperate economic situation meant that it was many years before the resurgent spirit of 'Herrijzend Nederland' was expressed in bricks and mortar.

What was called reconstruction was nearly always renewal. Usually it was cautious renewal but occasionally, as in Rotterdam, it was radical. Even so, all over the Netherlands the 'silent breakthrough' of a new approach to the city and city building was taking place, an approach based on an open city-form. Up until the Second World War most urban designers had seen a closed city-form in their mind's eye, the main exceptions being the functionalists who had been pushing for open subdivisions since the late 1920s. After the Second World War the closed city-form quietly disappeared from the urban planner's agenda. Even though the architecture was still traditional in many places, when it came to layout nearly all the reconstruction plans were dynamic, open and more than ever geared to a smooth through-flow of traffic.

The ease with which the open city-form gained the ascendency can be seen in the light of the fairly universal acceptance of the modern age as an inescapable reality. Modern urbanism was implicitly regarded as the logical or at least inevitable expression of this modern age. Apart from openness, post-war urbanism was characterized – once again – by an increase in scale. The breakthrough of this open and often large-scale city-form was nowhere more evident than in the reconstruction of Rotterdam. Work on the first reconstruction plan began a few weeks after the bombardment of May 1940. This plan, drawn up under the direction of W.G. Witteveen, while not based on a reconstruction of individual buildings, was intended to restore the general appearance of the city as it had existed up to 10 May 1940. Though the street pattern was adjusted on many points, there was no attempt to abandon the basic city-form in which individual lots were the norm. In Witteveen's eyes this plan was a continuation of the line he had already set out in his prewar designs for Rotterdam. A key feature of the design was the high degree of architectonic control. For each section of the development area a supervisor was appointed to keep a close eye on the external appearance.

In 1946, the Witteveen plan was officially replaced by the Basisplan voor Wederopbouw en Uitbreiding van Rotterdam (Basic Plan for the Reconstruction and Extension of Rotterdam) by C. van Traa. This plan was based on a reconstruction of the city using larger elements than Witteveen had envisaged and allowing much more latitude in architectural expression. At the moment when the Basic Plan came into force, however, work on the 'Witteveen reconstruction' had already commenced in several places in the city and today these areas stand out in the urban landscape as enclaves with a quite distinct idiom.

The approach to urban design in which a street elevation, instead of being designed as a unitary whole, is conceived as a coherent assemblage of individual buildings, each with its own character, continued to be followed until the mid-1950s in many places, including the cities of Nijmegen, Arnhem, Eindhoven and Groningen. Without attempting a full-blown historical reconstruction, this approach did make it possible to restore the scale that had existed prior to the devastation. The architecture, however, was in every case unmistakably new: sometimes distinctly modern in style and materials but more often traditional.

Although nobody said it in so many words, the war-time damage was viewed by some urban designers and architects as a blessing in disguise for it presented them with the opportunity of tackling a whole range of practical problems, many of which had defied solution for decades. The result was that all over the Netherlands urban designers set about trying to resolve old traffic problems, to relieve inner-city congestion, shift key areas and reorganize functions and activities. At the same time, planners found themselves confronted with at least as many new problems. In The Hague, for example, construction of the Scheveningen section of the Atlantic Wall had torn a long gash in the urban fabric. The open zone left behind by the demolition of this German coastal defence is still visible today in the change of urban scale near along Sportlaan, an area of relatively big, well-spaced buildings.

Seldom was there any attempt to recreate the prewar situation. Nowhere is this more evident than in Middelburg, which was heavily damaged in 1940. Although the city opted for restoration of the monumental abbey and the historic town hall, all other building can be seen as an exercise in cautious transformation in which atmosphere was considered more important than precise physical recreation. In a spatial intervention aimed at giving Middelburg even more atmosphere than it had enjoyed before, the axis, which ran right through the city core along the central square, was shifted slightly. Market Square is now at the junction of an inflected axis, a change of focus that has served to enhance the picturesque character of the townscape.

Middelburg was especially important to the Germans because they viewed the reconstruction plans as a test case for the repair of other damaged towns and villages, not just in the Netherlands but also elsewhere in occupied Europe. They were particularly keen that the reconstruction should convey the regional and typically Dutch character of Middelburg. The Dutch designers of reconstruction wanted the same thing, albeit for different reasons. The distinct Dutch character was for them, however implicitly, a form of resistance. The occupier did not take such a detailed interest in other reconstruction plans as in Middelburg, and certainly not at a concrete level. German architectural and urbanistic influences were confined to Christinakolonie in Heerlen. This estate of strictly regimented row housing was a purely German affair. Thanks in part to the building freeze that came into force in July 1942, it remained an exception.

Post-war reconstruction involved more than just repairing the torn fabric of villages, urban neighbourhoods and cities. Another huge task facing planners was the alleviation of the housing shortage. Whereas before the war many places had a surplus of housing in certain categories, for many decades after the Second World War the Netherlands had to contend with a chronic shortage of housing. The two main reasons for this were the destruction of a large number of dwellings between 1940 and 1945 and a post-war baby boom that led to an ever-increasing demand for accommodation. So as well as reconstructing the old neighbourhoods, planners were required to design new housing schemes. In Amsterdam this meant a resumption of the construction of the Westelijke Tuinsteden (western garden suburbs) included in the 1934 General Extension Plan (AUP). A modest start had already been made before the war, and after the war Slotermeer was built followed by Geuzenveld. In Rotterdam W. van Tijen oversaw the planning of several schemes including Zuidwijk, where construction began at the end of the 1940s. A few years after the war, work began on the design of the neighbouring Pendrecht district under the supervision of the head of the town planning department, L. Stam-Beese. The same thing was happening on a proportional scale in smaller communities. Everywhere new extensions were being planned.

The design of Zuidwijk was included as a model plan in De Stad der Toekomst, de Toekomst der Stad (The city of the future, the future of the city). This book, one of the products of the (enforced) period of reflection that the war represented for many professionals in the absence of concrete commissions, gave expression to the 'neighbourhood' concept: a social approach to the city focusing on the organic relationship between the multitude and the individual. Architecture and urban design were seen as important tools for mitigating the 'chaotic, mechanical, materialistic and homogenizing' nature of 'modern life'. 'The problem then will be how to offer city dwellers a community that is sufficiently small and orderly that they can feel at home there.' The solution was an articulated city, made up of small neighbourhoods which together formed districts, which in turn merged to form boroughs. The idea was not to 'use the neighbourhood organization to break the big city up into a number of small, isolated provincial towns. Quite the contrary'. But the city as a whole was viewed as so big that individuals might easily feel lost in it. The neighbourhood, with some twenty thousand inhabitants, was the ideal size for the development of social life.

The idea that the big city was too amorphous and too fragmented was approached from a different angle by a group of Amsterdam architects. In Bouwen van Woning tot Stad (Building from dwelling to city), a study written during the war, A. Staal, A. Komter, A. Boeken and Zanstra, Giesen & Sijmons outlined their alternative to the Amsterdam AUP which they criticized as a shapeless plan offering 'too little scope for architecture'. Unlike the 'analytical' AUP, their proposal, with its 'liveliness and humanity' was 'an outline for an architectonic plan', a huge new canal zone thrown around the existing city. 'As the city was laid out and built in 1610, so it ends.'

Although this plan was never considered seriously, many people would have agreed with its two main premises: that the city should and could have a self-contained form and that designers should provide an urban environment in which the individual would not feel lost. During the 1950s and part of the 1960s these were the implicit premises underlying numerous urban design schemes, especially those for new residential areas.

C.I.A. Stam-Beese Kleinpolder, Rotterdam (1945)

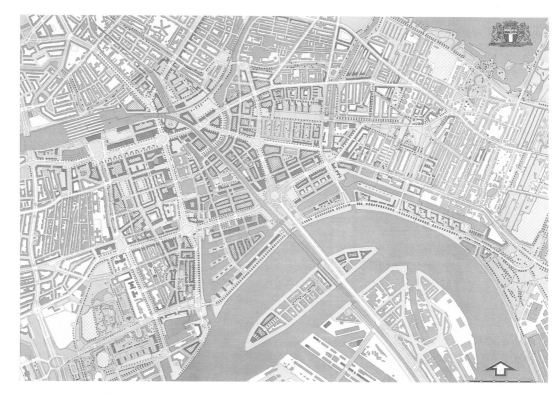

P. Verhagen   pre-1940 and post-war reconstruction plan for Middelburg (1940)

C. van Traa, Opbouw Rotterdam   basic reconstruction plan for inner-city, Rotterdam (1946)

Leuvehaven in the 1950s, Rotterdam

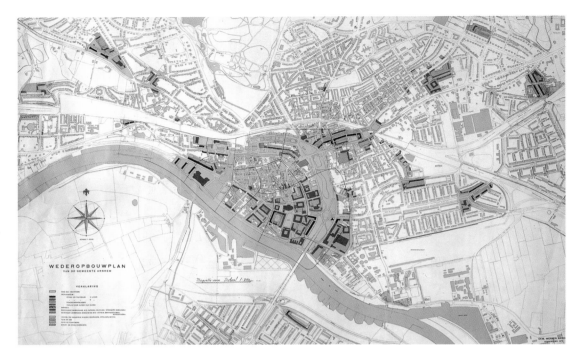

J.A. van der Laan   basic reconstruction plan, Arnhem (1947)

reconstruction plan Gele Rijdersplein, Arnhem (c. 1955)

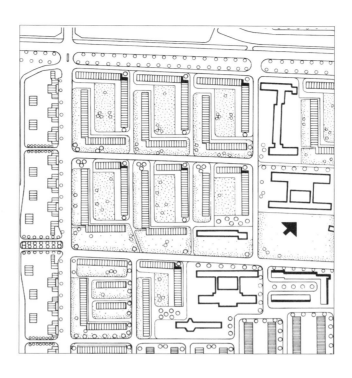

B. Merkelbach & C.J.F. Karsten, M. Stam, B. Merkelbach & P. Elling housing Frankendaal garden suburb,
Amsterdam East (1947-1951)

76

W.M. Dudok   Oostplein reconstruction plan, The Hague (1946)

W.M. Dudok   Bezuidenhout reconstruction plan, left Oostplein, right neighbourhood centre,

The Hague (1945-1952)

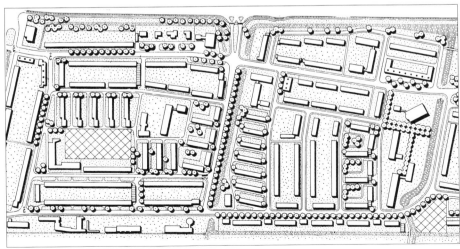

W. Bruin   Thamerdal housing estate, Uithoorn (1950)

illustration Neighbourhood Concept (1946-1947)

W. van Tijen, E.F. Groosman   urban design plan and housing Zuidwijk, Rotterdam (1948-1952)

W. van Tijen, E.F. Groosman   urban design plan and housing Zuidwijk, Rotterdam (1948-1952)

80

J. Wils   housing Blijdorp, Rotterdam (1942)

J.J.P. Oud   competition design for Hofplein, Rotterdam (1942-1943)

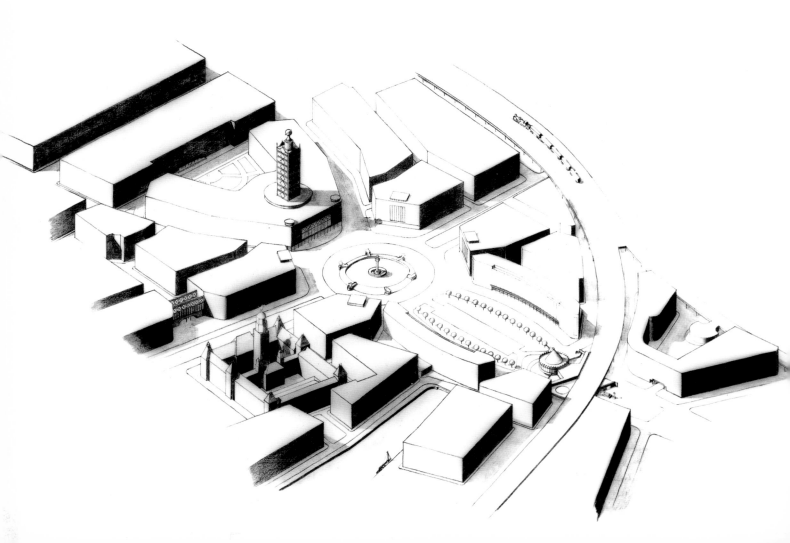

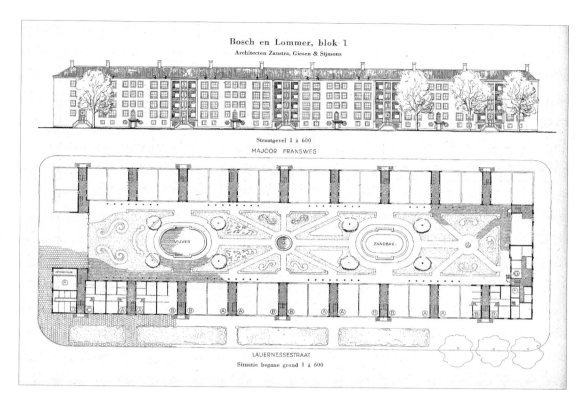

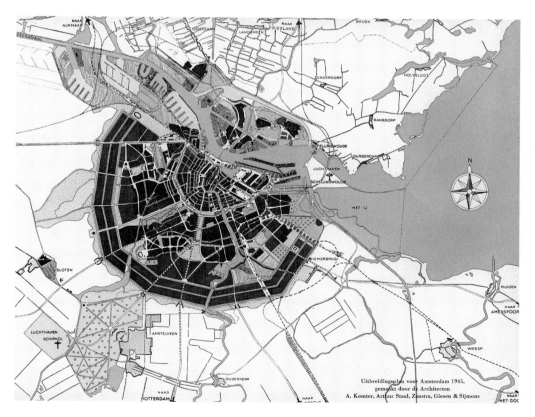

P. Zanstra, J.H.L. Giesen, K.L. Sijmons housing Bos en Lommer, Amsterdam (1945)

A. Staal, A Komter, A. Boeken, P. Zanstra, J.H.L. Giesen, K.L. Sijmons alternative extension plan for Amsterdam (1945)

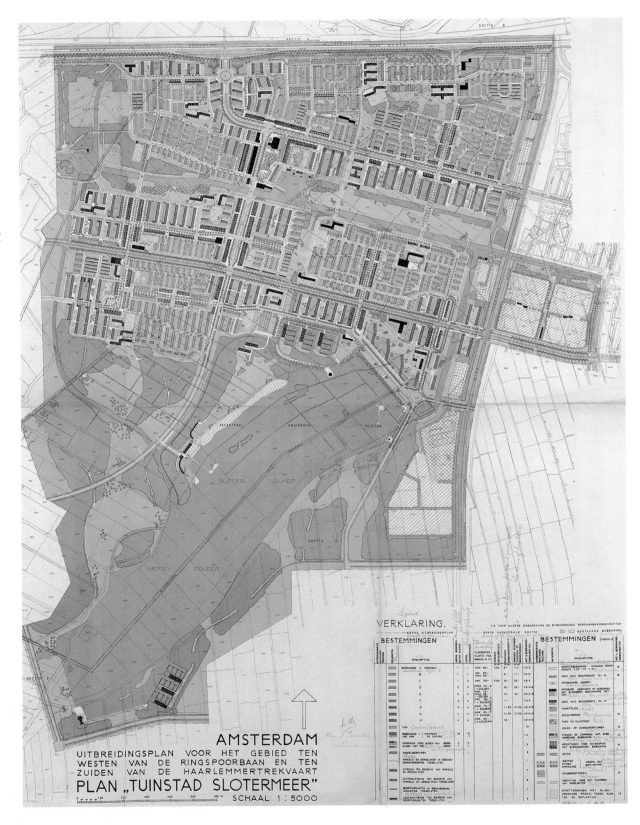

Public Works Department   urban design plan garden city Slotermeer, Amsterdam (1939)

83

Public Works Department   A. Meerwaldpark housing Slotermeer, Amsterdam (1950s)

F.P.J. Peutz   housing complex, Breda (1952)

1950-1960

The open city

The 1950s were a time of reconstruction and expansion. By the beginning of the decade the Dutch economy had regained its prewar level and from that moment onwards prosperity increased, tentatively at first, then gathering pace as the decade progressed. But while the economy was rebuilt within a few short years, reconstruction of the built environment took considerably longer.

In most of the war-damaged cities construction work continued steadily into the 1960s. In Rotterdam, for example, where the Lijnbaan shopping centre and Central Station were completed in 1956 and De Bijenkorf department store in 1958, De Doelen concert hall was not finished until 1966. Elsewhere too it was many years before the fabric of cities and villages was fully repaired. Moreover, reconstruction was only part of the building task. About half of the building production in these years consisted of additional housing stock. So severe was the post-war housing shortage that it was designated 'public enemy number one'. There was scarcely a municipality in the Netherlands that was not busy building new housing estates. In the 1950s these were for the most part made up of low and medium-rise row housing. Some of the larger schemes made use of high-rise blocks, but the heyday of the gallery-access block, six to fifteen storeys high, was still a decade away. Most of the new estates built in the 1950s were relatively small-scale, with at best one or two vertical accents, such as the modest tower blocks along the periphery of Soesterkwartier in Amersfoort, designed by D. Zuiderhoek. Soesterkwartier differed from many other 1950s housing estates in that its spatial layout was not ruled by a strict orthogonality. One of the earliest examples of such a squared layout, and the model for countless other new districts, was Pendrecht in Rotterdam. Designed by L. Stam-Beese in her capacity as municipal town planner, the Pendrecht spatial layout consisted of an ensemble of row housing repeated over and over again. By deploying this 'stamp' in mirror form or rotated it was possible to introduce controlled variation into the basic configuration. Each stamp constituted what the designers called a 'cluster', a mixed composition of low and medium rise suitable for housing a heterogeneous population: elderly people and families in the low-rise blocks and young families, couples and singles in the flats, exactly as prescribed by the 'neighbourhood' concept.

The neighbourhood concept was at the local level what spatial planning was at the national level: an instrument for shaping society. Historically, government policy in the field of town and country planning had been geared to controlling development and steering it in the right direction. After the Second World War planning was increasingly used to stimulate development. The reclamation of large parts of the IJsselmeer created new land for settlement and agriculture while the policy of industrial decentralization actively encouraged companies to settle outside the Randstad conglomeration.

This proactive approach was encapsulated in several, mainly economically-inspired, policy documents relating to decentralization and in Het Westen en Overig Nederland (The West and the rest of the Netherlands, 1958), the first such formulation of national spatial planning intentions and the prelude to the more specific Nota inzake de ruimtelijke ordening (Report on spatial planning) of 1960. According to the authors of Het Westen en Overig Nederland, a more even dispersal of population and industry was needed in order to reduce the differences between the Randstad and the rest of the country and to prevent the Randstad from becoming too congested. The report was the first of many warnings that the western part of the Netherlands was in danger of becoming overpopulated. Apart from nationwide dispersal, the authors of Het Westen en Overig Nederland also advanced the notion of 'overspill' whereby new and existing towns in and near the Randstad would be called upon to absorb some of the population increase. The towns they had in mind were Zoetermeer, Nieuwegein, Alkmaar, Hoorn, Lelystad and other new towns in the Flevo Polder and in the projected (but never realized) Markerwaard Polder, plus a large expansion area south of Rotterdam.

One of the effects of decentralization was to turn the village of Emmen (some 120 km northeast of Amsterdam) into a town. Emmen was designated an official development area and the prospect of government subsidies was dangled in front of companies prepared to set up business there. The arrival in 1949 of the Enkalon synthetic fibres factory marked the beginning of a large-scale expansion programme. The first new residential area, Emmermeer, was designed separately. It was not until the early 1960s that N. de Boer drew up a comprehensive structure plan for Emmen which provided for the phased development of self-contained districts. Thanks to its wooded setting, the new town of Emmen presented from the outset a very different picture from many other new villages, towns and expansion areas that were projected onto flat, bare and in many cases reclaimed land. A classic example of the latter are the towns and villages built in the Northeast Polder. Ranged around the largest municipality, Emmeloord, is a ring of villages almost entirely dependent on this town for their amenities. Lining the connecting roads are farms, often with additional housing for contract workers. This orderly composition of farm, village and town can be viewed as a polder version of the neighbourhood concept.

As construction began in the Northeast Polder, C. van Eesteren was working on a development plan for the neighbouring polder of East Flevoland, including a design for what was to become its largest urban centre, Lelystad. Leading modernist that he was, Van Eesteren chose to give the new town a linear layout. The advantage of the linear model over the concentric model is its capacity for growth: a linear city can be more easily extended as the need arises. Among other things, it meant that Lelystad could begin life with a town centre capable of developing in step with the population. The city was intended to function as an expansion tank for the overcrowded, northern part of the Randstad, in particular the Amsterdam area. Similar motives were behind the masterplan drawn up by Van den Broek & Bakema for a large new town in North Kennemerland, the open area between Zaanstreek (the industrial region either side of the River Zaan) and Alkmaar. The plan was never realized, mainly because the twelve municipalities who had jointly commissioned it were unable to reach agreement. In the event, this may have been a blessing in disguise since the increase in population turned out to be a good deal less than predicted. The North Kennemerland plan displays a form of urbanization in which the open housing estate has been extended to form an open city. As such, it can be seen as an enlargement of the urban development model of the period.

The open city that resulted from the construction of spacious estates of open row housing was ideally suited to motorized traffic. From relatively modest beginnings, the number private and commercial vehicles in the Netherlands tripled between 1950 and 1960 to over six hundred thousand. The expansion of the highway network kept pace with this increase, growing from 121 kilometres in 1950 to 351 kilometres in 1960. The volume of traffic increased dramatically both inside and outside the built-up area. Although this was seen as a problem, the prevailing view was that the city should adapt to the motor car rather than the other way round. Interventions in towns and villages aimed at facilitating the through-flow of traffic were based on this notion. Though many of these traffic corridors had been conceived in the 1950s, some in the context of a reconstruction plan, it often took until the 1960s or even the 1970s before they were finally built. One example of such traffic corridors is the wide boulevard built over the route of the once narrow Weesperstraat in Amsterdam. In Utrecht, the German traffic engineer M. Feuchtinger drew up a traffic plan for two concentric ring roads. The inner one required the filling in of a large part of the Catharijnesingel. In the end only a small section of the canal was turned into a motorway in the 1960s, an intervention that is due to be reversed early in the 21st century when the Utrecht Centre Project (UCP) is realized. Comparable plans for traffic arteries were put forward in Tilburg, again for inner and outer orbital roads, and in The Hague, where the Department of Reconstruction and Urban Development presented a plan in 1952 for an inner ring road around the city and a 'shunting route' to connect Kijkduin with Scheveningen via Rijswijk. The latter idea culminated, among other things, in the Utrechtsebaan, a motorway that debouches into the heart of The Hague.

The motor car was also amply provided for in the new urban expansion areas, as can be see for example on the outskirts of Leeuwarden where the vast Europaplein roundabout offers motorists a majestic entry to the city. Europaplein is also a typical 1950s name, for it was at this point that the continent started to occupy an important place in public consciousness and thus also in spatial planning. The decade in which maps of Europe centred on the Netherlands started to appear, was also marked by the dawning realization that from now on planning in the Netherlands would have to be seen in an international perspective. The First Report on Spatial Planning placed the development of the 'rim cities of Randstad Holland' in the wider context of the Rhine-Ruhr region and the 'big Belgian-French agglomerations' in which the Netherlands was assigned a 'gateway role between Western Europe and the world's oceans'. Europoort (European gateway) was thus a fitting name for the planned expansion of the Rotterdam harbour. The growth and relocation of port activities began in the 1950s with the development of the Botlek area. There followed plans for the reclamation of the Maasvlakte, the designated site of Europoort. The main users of the new harbour areas were the oil refineries and later on the container operators. These industries not only needed a lot of space but also required deep navigation channels to accommodate ever-larger oil tankers and container vessels.

Apart from changes wrought by traffic corridors and new infrastructure, the cities were also drastically transformed by redevelopment and slum clearance, terms which referred to the demolition of old, often rundown inner-city areas. 'Redevelopment' usually meant wholesale demolition followed by the construction of new buildings that had little or nothing in common with what had gone before. This continued to be standard practice until about 1970.

One exception to this general rule was the redevelopment of the Stokstraat area in the centre of Maastricht which sought to retain the historical structure and buildings. But even though the architecture and urban fabric were spared, the Stokstraat redevelopment was still, in social terms at least, an act of demolition. The inhabitants were branded asocial and relocated on the outskirts of the city, some in a special 'domestic training' neighbourhood to learn civilized behaviour under the watchful eye of a (usually female) supervisor. They did not return to their old neighbourhood after it had been rebuilt.

88

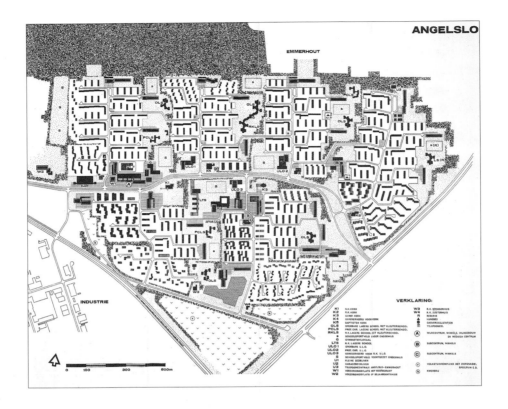

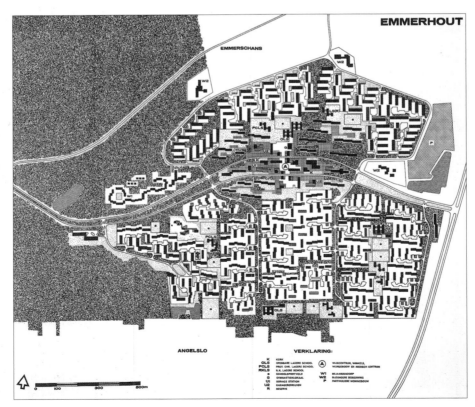

N.A. de Boer with **A.J.M. de Jong, Public Works Department Emmen**   urban design plan for Angelslo, Emmen (1960)

N.A. de Boer, A.J.M. de Jong   urban design plan for Emmerhout, Emmen (1960)

T. Strikwerda   housing Angelslo, Emmen (1960-1969)

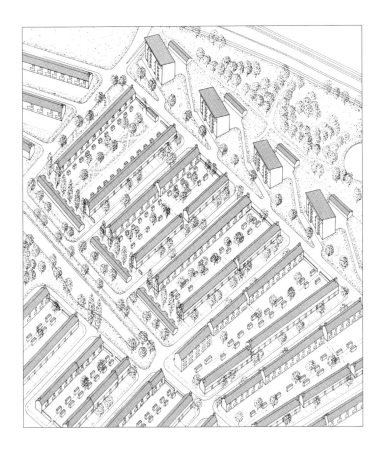

D. Zuiderhoek Public Works Department Amersfoort with **A.H. Rooimans** Soesterkwartier, Amersfoort (1947-1953)

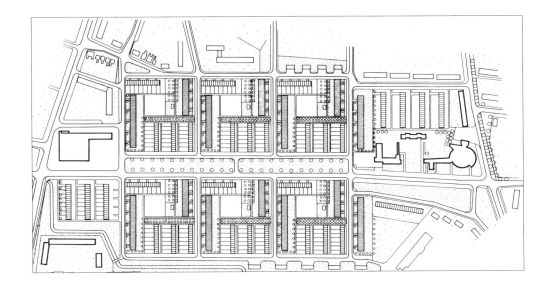

Van den Broek & Bakema   Klein Driene, Hengelo (1951-1959)

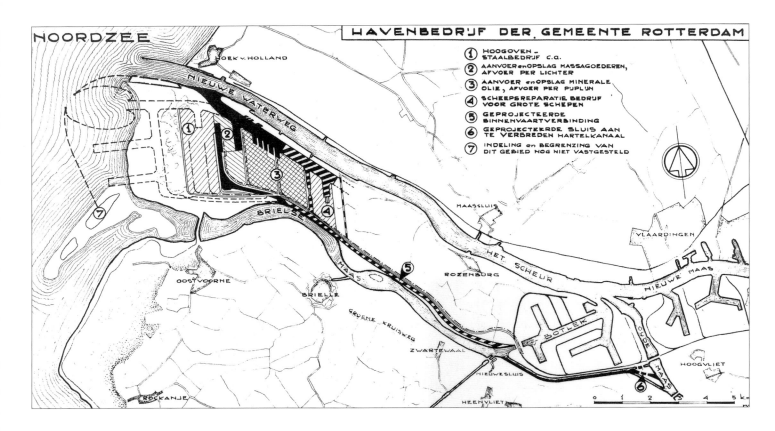

NOORDZEE

HAVENBEDRIJF DER GEMEENTE ROTTERDAM

1 HOOGOVEN-STAALBEDRIJF c.a.
2 AANVOER en OPSLAG MASSAGOEDEREN, AFVOER PER LICHTER
3 AANVOER en OPSLAG MINERALE OLIE, AFVOER PER PIJPLIJN
4 SCHEEPSREPARATIE BEDRIJF VOOR GROTE SCHEPEN
5 GEPROJECTEERDE BINNENVAARTVERBINDING
6 GEPROJECTEERDE SLUIS AAN TE VERBREDEN HARTELKANAAL
7 INDELING en BEGRENZING VAN DIT GEBIED NOG NIET VASTGESTELD

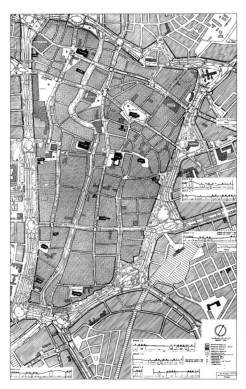

Rotterdam Port Authority   Europoort plan with Botlekgebied under construction, Rotterdam (1957)

M.E. Feuchtinger   traffic plan, Utrecht (1958-1959)

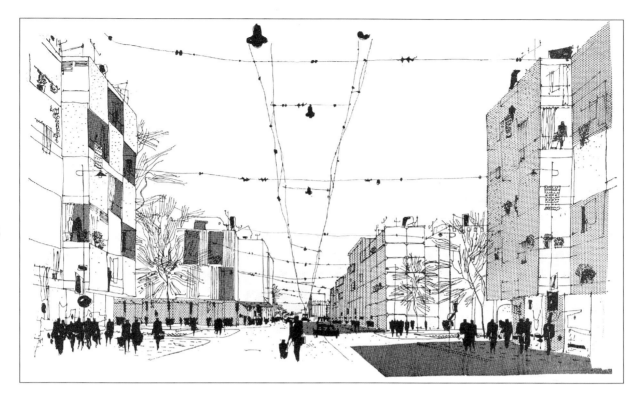

93

C. Wegener Sleeswijk   sketch of future Weesperstraat streetscape, Amsterdam (c. 1960)

Van den Broek & Bakema   regional plan, Noord Kennemerland (1956-1959)

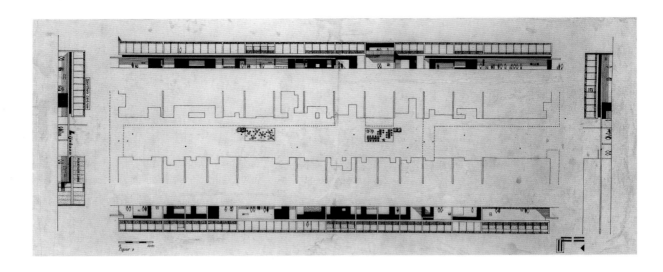

94

Van den Broek & Bakema   De Lijnbaan shopping centre, Rotterdam (1948-1953)

Hofplein in the 1950s, Rotterdam

De 8 urban design plan, Nagele (1954-1957) / **Van den Broek & Bakema** Dutch Reformed Church, Nagele (1958-1962)

W. van Tijen with **M. Boon** development plan and housing Geuzenveld, Amsterdam (1953-1958)

Public Works Department Rotterdam   open row housing Alexanderpolder, Rotterdam (1953-1956)

Public Works Department   spatial masterplan Grootstal, Nijmegen (c. 1960)

Europaplein, Leeuwarden (1953-1954)

J.F. Berghoef housing Sloterhof, Amsterdam (1955-1960)

C.I.A. Stam-Beese housing and development plan Pendrecht, Rotterdam (1949-1953)

Department of Town Planning, F.C. Dingemans   Stokstraat, Maastricht (1954-1973)

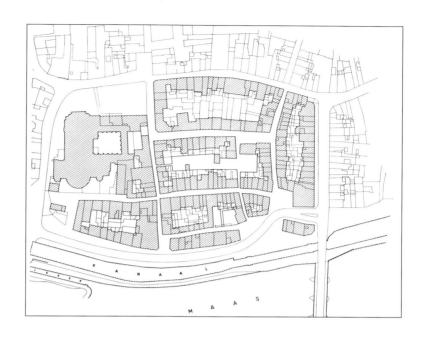

Department of Town Planning, F.C. Dingemans Stokstraat, Maastricht (1954-1973)

W. Wissing optional floor plan housing, Alphen aan den Rijn (1957)

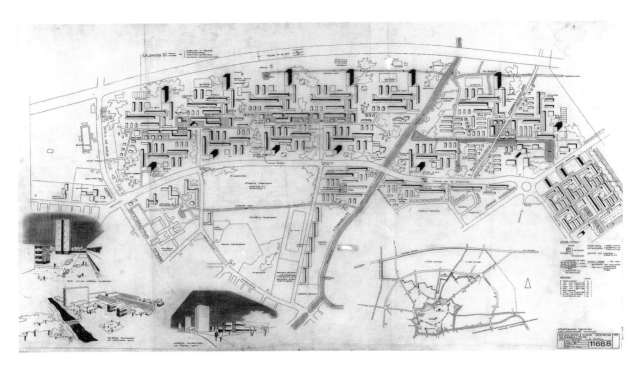

Van den Broek & Bakema development plan Bilgaard/Lekkumerend, Leeuwarden-North (1957-1959/1962-1972)

B. van Grunsven, H. Schröder, G. Rietveld housing Hoograven, Utrecht (1954-1957)

P. Zanstra, A.W. Gmelig Meyling, P.J. de Clerq Zubli housing Mariahoeve, The Hague (1957-1964)

1960-1970

Megastructures

Urban planning strategies in the 1960s differed little from those of previous years. Many of the new residential developments continued to be based on the same principles as in the preceding decade: a strict orthogonal layout with a mix of low, medium and high-rise in line with the precepts of the neighbourhood concept. Variations on this theme did, however, start to appear in this decade, as for example in the Rotterdam suburb of Ommoord, in Bijlmermeer in Amsterdam and in Angelslo in Emmen. A typical 1960s phenomenon was the megastructure, architectonic complexes the size of an urban borough and even, on occasion, of a small town. Hoog Catharijne in the centre of Utrecht was one of the few such megastructures to actually be built.

The 1960s also marked the formal introduction of national planning. The first Nota inzake de ruimtelijke ordening (Report on Spatial Planning) was published in 1960. Five years later the Spatial Planning Act came into force and was quickly followed in 1966 by a Second Report on Spatial Planning (Tweede Nota over de Ruimtelijke Ordening). The result of all this activity was a nationwide system of spatial planning with firm legal and administrative foundations. There was legislation, a range of planning bodies at local, regional and national level and a government policy enshrined in spatial planning policy documents. The first Report of 1960 was in large part a rehearsal of what had been said in the 1958 report Het Westen en Overig Nederland. The central theme was a more even distribution of population and prosperity, aimed at reducing the disparity between the Randstad region and 'the rest of the country' where the population density was ten times lower.

The 1960 report paid special attention to the non-urbanized area: 'The most common spatial problem relates to agricultural land. Farming takes up by far the largest area of land in our country; on top of this, the farming community, especially in the North, the East and in Zeeland, accounts for a relatively large proportion of the workforce.' But many farms were so small that they failed to meet the 'demands of modern business'. Accordingly, the document called for land consolidation in the interests of rationalization. Implementation of this policy had a profound effect on the landscape which was increasingly determined by large, regular parcels of agricultural land.

Towards the end of the report, the government summed up a number of policy objectives. One of these was to try to stimulate 'public interest' and to promote a 'fruitful interaction' between government and society, with particular value being attached to 'initiatives originating in the business community'. Whereas for decades the government had taken the lead in spatial planning, now private enterprise was being invited to take the initiative, which it did. The 1960s saw the emergence of big property developers like Bredero, who was responsible for Hoog Catharijne, and Zwolsman, who came up with a proposal (the Nervi Plan) for the Spuikwartier in The Hague.

By the time the Second Report on Spatial Planning appeared six years later, a specific concept had been devised for the government's policy on dispersion. Dubbed 'clustered dispersal' it steered a middle course between concentration and dispersion. The strategy was a trade-off between the desirability of a more even spread of population and the need to ensure that the country was not swallowed up by uncontrolled suburban sprawl. Hence the decision to concentrate growth as much as possible in a limited number of municipalities.

The Second Report also broke new ground by including a section on the environment under the heading 'Air, noise, radiation'. The old notion of recreational green space as a buffer zone between housing and industry was abandoned and air traffic was identified as a possible source of noise nuisance. The acknowledgement of the environmental issue was not the only about-face in spatial planning thinking, for it was in the early 1960s that planners also started to perceive population growth as a major problem. The most recent forecast of a doubling of the Dutch population (from eleven to twenty million) by the year 2000 caused great consternation. Yet, at the same time, the 1960s were a period of unprecedented faith in society's ability to solve all its technical and social problems by rational means. The Delta Works begun in the wake of the disastrous flooding of 1953 were proof of this, as were other major construction projects in Amsterdam, Rotterdam, The Hague and Utrecht.

The largest project undertaken in Amsterdam was a planning experiment involving the construction of a whole new borough in the Bijlmermeer, an area to the southeast of Amsterdam. Heralded as the City of Tomorrow, the Bijlmer, as it came to be known to friend and foe alike, was designed by the Public Works Department under the direction of S. Nassuth. The plan was invariably presented as a continuation of Van Eesteren's General Extension Plan for Amsterdam (AUP) drawn up in the 1930s. The AUP had been designed as a 'final plan' but it now transpired that the city needed more space for housing than had been foreseen before the war. The Bijlmer design was in keeping with the tradition of the neighbourhood concept, with a clear articulation of borough, district, neighbourhood and with facilities designed to turn the housing block into a community. The metro, which was not completed until many years later, connected the Bijlmer to the rest of Amsterdam and as the element linking the various parts of the scheme together, it symbolized the unity aspired to in the City of Tomorrow. Because of the rigorously enforced decision to separate motorized traffic from all other forms of traffic, the traditional street disappeared as a planning tool in the Bijlmer. With its tower blocks disposed in a park-like setting criss-crossed by foot and cycle paths, the Bijlmer is an extreme elaboration of the 1930s modernist concept of living in green surroundings. The characteristic, honeycomb-shape of the apartment blocks was intended to generate internal courts with an intimacy lacking in orthogonal row housing. A similar purpose informed the high-rise buildings in the Rotterdam suburb of Ommoord designed by L. Stam-Beese. After the Alexander polder, planned in the 1950s and realized in the 1960s, Ommoord was the next extension of Rotterdam in an easterly direction. The earliest plans reveal a straightforwardly orthogonal layout but in the final design the tower blocks were hook-shaped in plan around an obtuse angle. According to Stam-Beese, this deviation from the right angle suggested 'a desirable "personal" space rather than simply "in-between" space. This inflection turns a utilitarian linear measure into a spatial experience'. Moreover, once the trees were full-grown, 'the austerity and height of the elevations' would be hidden from sight: 'The field of vision will be defined by the alternation of tall groups of trees and open lawns, of peaceful sitting areas and lively playgrounds, of water and gently winding footpaths; all elements that in character, size and shape have been familiar to us since childhood.'

Another very different design that also eschewed the classic street is Angelslo in Emmen, by N. de Boer and A.J.M. de Jong. The masterplan drawn

up for Emmen in 1963 was based on the concept of the 'open green city' which can be seen as a continuation of the organic tradition of designers like Witteveen, who had embraced the idea of copious urban green space way back in the 1920s. Angelslo was the first residential development to be based on the principle of the 'home zone' (woonerf), an idea that was enthusiastically adopted in municipalities throughout the Netherlands in the 1970s and which is now catching on in the United Kingdom. In home zones pedestrians and cyclists take priority over vehicles which are restricted to little more than walking pace.

Physical separation of different types of traffic was a major theme of the Hoog Catharijne complex in the centre of Utrecht, designed by urban planner H.T. Vink, the architects K. van der Gaast, G.J. van der Grinten, B. van Kasteel and K.F.G. Spruit (who was concurrently working elsewhere in Utrecht on the huge Overvecht housing estate in collaboration with the local Department of Urban Development and W. Wissing). Encompassing shops, offices, theatres and a public transport interchange, Hoog Catharijne was promoted as a refurbishment of the 'unpretentious' development around the station. The idea was that the large, raised shopping mall, initially conceived as open but eventually realized as a wholly enclosed space, would serve to unite railway station, exhibition complex and city centre, while at the same time separating the pedestrian shopper from all other forms of traffic. Designed to halt the drift of businesses away from the centre of Utrecht, the 250,000 m^2 complex was a wholly private initiative organized by the Bredero development company.

Hoog Catharijne is typical of the general increase in scale during the 1960s and of the notion held by many architects and urban designers at that time, that it should be possible to combine building and city in complexes for which Van den Broek & Bakema coined the term 'architecture-urbanism'. Examples of such complexes are that practice's Pampus Plan, an extension to Amsterdam for 250,000 inhabitants, and Hydrobiopolis, a terraced city off the coast of The Hague designed by the husband and wife team of E. & L. Hartsuyker.

Such grandiose schemes are merely the most extreme examples from a period when planners everywhere were preparing for large-scale expansion. In Rotterdam, for example, three municipal departments (Urban Development,

Public Works and the Port Authority) joined forces to produce Plan 2000+ in 1969. It envisaged Rotterdam and the surrounding area merging to form one big urban agglomeration, from Gouda in the north to Goeree-Overflakkee in the south, where a new town (Grevelingenstad) would rise to accommodate an additional 500,000 inhabitants (scarcely fewer than the total population of Rotterdam in 2000). The Randstad cities were not the only ones anticipating steep, short-term growth. The town of Emmen was expected to rise to 200,000 inhabitants, while projections for the overspill town of Lelystad spoke of 100,000 inhabitants, a prediction that has yet to be fulfilled.

For The Hague, shut in between the sea and neighbouring municipalities, expansion was a big problem. Neither building off-shore nor annexation was a realistic proposition. In addition to lack of space, the city also had to contend with poor accessibility and a number of rundown neighbourhoods dating from the beginning of the century. In the 1960s various designs were made which tackled these problems rigorously. None of these plans was ever executed in its entirety but all over The Hague traces can be found of the major urban interventions conceived in this decade: the motorways penetrating deep into the heart of the city (the Utrechtsebaan and Prins Bernhardviaduct), Central Station, originally planned underground but because of the high cost involved eventually built at street level, and the Spuikwartier, the scene of almost uninterrupted redevelopment from the 1960s to the beginning of the twenty-first century. On the other hand, plans to transform Schilderswijk into a high-rise housing estate foundered on the increasingly vociferous protest of local residents. In the late 1960s similar plans were produced for old inner-city areas in Amsterdam and Rotterdam but in a period when citizens were less and less inclined to go along with whatever the authorities thought was good for them, these too met with growing public resistance. This led to the emergence in the 1970s of a fundamentally different strategy. The large-scale redevelopment plans of the 1960s made way for a more circumspect approach which eventually resulted in urban renewal in existing urban areas and to a culture of home zones, low-rise housing and small-scale development in the new areas.

Van den Broek & Bakema   housing 't Groene Hart, Kampen (1965-1967)

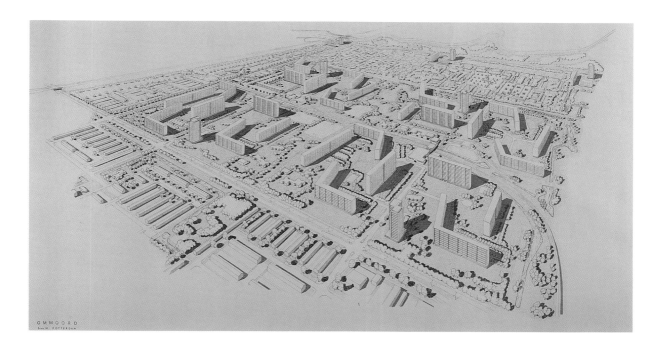

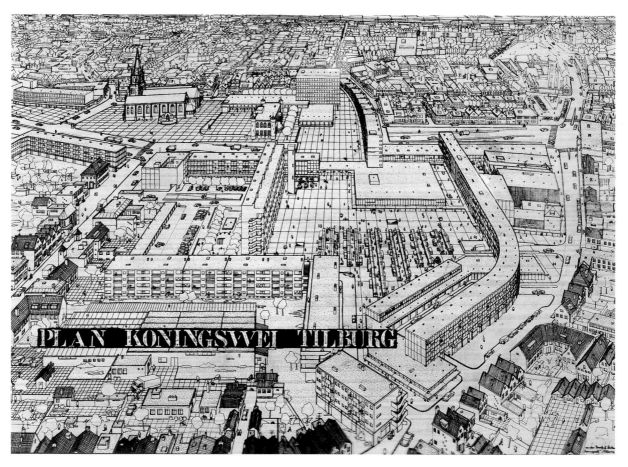

C.I.A. Stam-Beese housing and development plan Ommoord, Rotterdam (1962-1977)

Van den Broek & Bakema plan for Koningswei, Tilburg (1969)

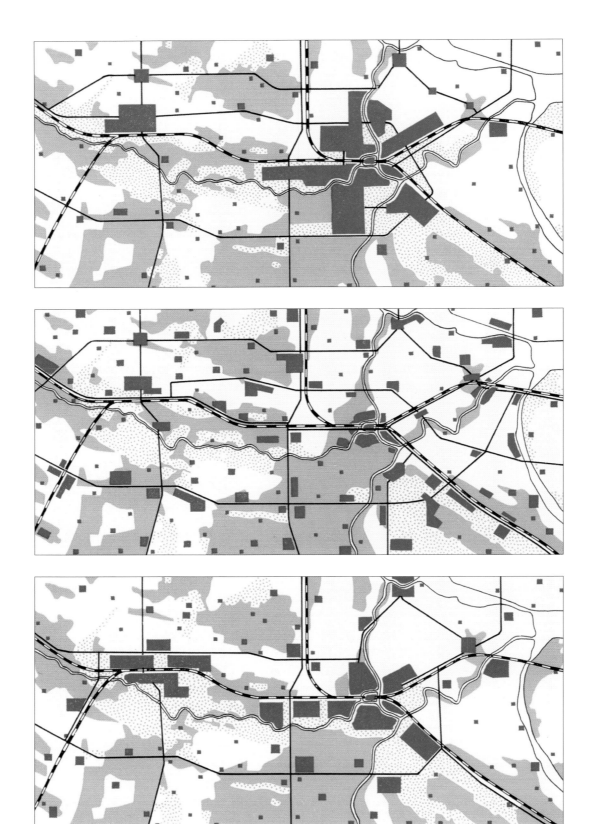

three urbanization scenarios in accordance with the Second Report: concentration, dispersal
and clustered dispersal (1966)

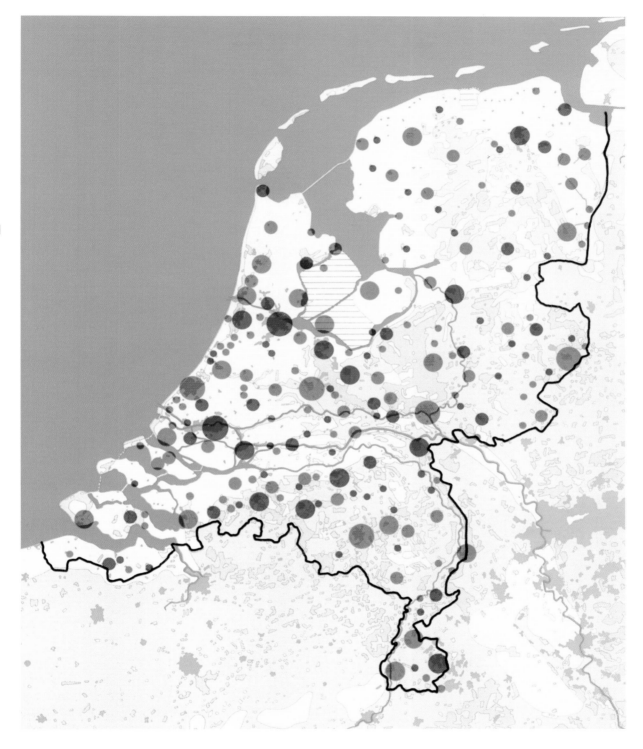

map of population distribution c. 2000 (1966)

WOONBEBOUWING
CENTRA
DIENSTENSECTOR EN CENTRUMFUNCTIES
INDUSTRIE
MARGE INDUSTRIETERREIN
SPORT EN VOLKSTUINEN
PARK EN GROENVOORZIENING
+ BEGRAAFPLAATS

LELYSTAD
STRUCTUURPLAN
SCHAAL 1:10.000
PROF. C. VAN EESTEREN

C. van Eesteren development phases and structure plan, Lelystad (1964)

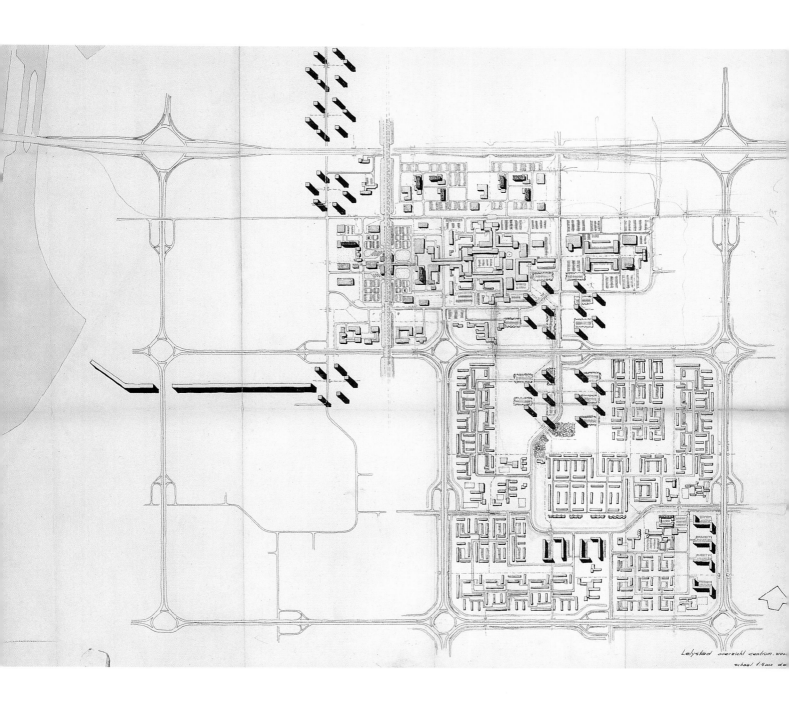

Lelystad overzicht centrum woo...
schaal 1:5000 d...

C. van Eesteren development plan, Lelystad (1966)

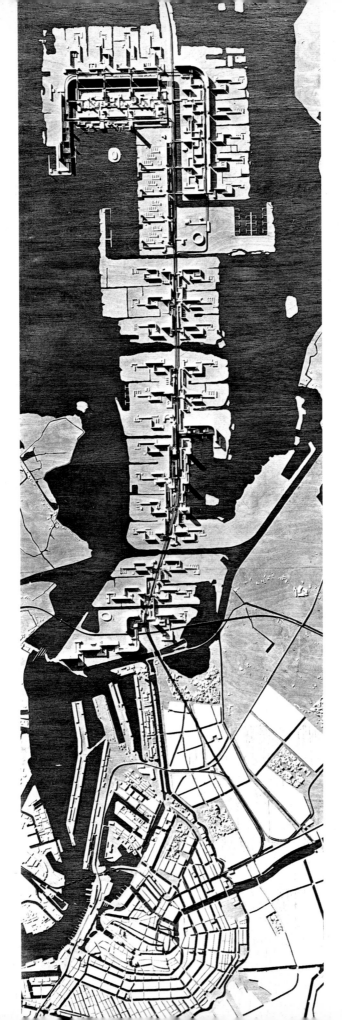

114

Van den Broek & Bakema urban design study Pampus, Amsterdam (1964)

116

H.T. Vink, G.J. van der Grinten, B. van Kasteel, K.F.G. Spruit Hoog Catharijne, Utrecht (1962-1981)

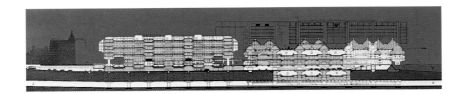

118

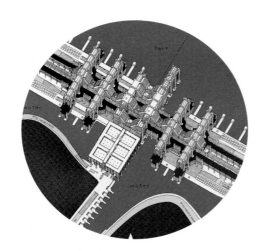

C. Weeber Prix de Rome design (1966)

F.J. van Gool Buikslotermeer development, Amsterdam (1963-1966)

Zoetermeer Development Task Force, S.J. Embden, R.H. Fledderus, W.F. Schut   structure plan, Zoetermeer (1964)

Department of Town Planning, G.S. Nassuth   development plan Bijlmermeer, Amsterdam (1962-1971)

Department of Town Planning, G.S. Nassuth development plan Bijlmermeer, Amsterdam (1962-1971)

1970-1980

The sociable city

By the end of the 1960s large-scale projects like the Bijlmer and Hoog Catharijne had become the target of increasing criticism. Small-scale development and sociability were the new watchwords in urban design. A negative attitude developed towards the city which was increasingly seen as an inhospitable cement and asphalt jungle. The contemporary ideal was a rural, village-like environment. The popularity of the woonerf (home zone) and the new rage for a converted farmhouse in the country can be seen as expressions of an anti-urban mentality that also had far-reaching consequences for spatial planning: there was a demand for rural peace and quiet in urban environments, too, and high-rise was completely out of favour. Urban designs with pretensions to grandeur were pretty well non-existent. Broad, straight thoroughfares made way for a 'winding, forty-five degree regime' and wherever possible the motor car was severely circumscribed or banished altogether. This was the time of by-passes and traffic circulation plans aimed at discouraging motorists. An echo of this is to be found in the Third Report on Spatial Planning which appeared from 1973 onwards in a series of working papers, sectional reports, development plans and key planning decisions, in itself a faithful reflection of the prevailing consultative culture. The suggestion that bicycle use should be encouraged was mooted for the first time in this report.

The swing away from large-scale, car-based urban planning to small-scale designs tailored to people walking, cycling and playing, is epitomized in the history of the Prins Bernhard viaduct in The Hague. Less than ten years after this piece of motorway had been driven deep into the heart of city, it was decided to demolish part of it. Similar abortive traffic plans can be found in other Dutch cities. In Utrecht a section of motorway leading from no place to nowhere runs under Hoog Catharijne, while in Amsterdam the road running along the Haarlemmerhouttuinen district, which was to have become a motorway, is still just a very busy dual carriageway road.

The anti-urban mentality of the 1970s had a direct impact on the population of the big cities which began to decline in these years, chiefly as a result of the exodus to medium-sized municipalities. At the same time there was a complementary drift away from rural areas. The government's response to this suburbanization process continued to be based on the policy of clustered dispersal as set out in the Second Report. In practical terms this resulted in the 'growth centres' policy that made its appearance in 1972. The municipalities designated as centres of growth – Alkmaar, Almere (still on the drawing board at this stage), Capelle aan den IJssel, Hellevoetsluis, Helmond, Hoorn, Houten, Huizen,

Lelystad, Nieuwegein (an amalgamation of Jutphaas and Vreeswijk), Purmerend, Spijkenisse and Zoetermeer – were intended to absorb the exodus from the cities plus any increase in population. The result was that these small towns and villages were rapidly transformed into large urban areas, albeit in most cases minus the range of activities typical of a true city. Growth centres were often rather one-sided developments, consisting mainly of residential areas occupied by commuters. There was – and is – little employment to be had; shops, restaurants, theatres and cinemas were in short supply. For work and urban amenities the inhabitants of these places (often referred to as dormitory towns) had to rely on big cities in the area, a situation that only began to change in the late 1980s. The provision of public transport also lagged behind development: the express tram from Utrecht to Nieuwegein, the train between The Hague and Zoetermeer and the train from Amsterdam to Lelystad and Almere all arrived much later than originally planned.

Lelystad, which can be seen as one of the last examples of modernist urban design in the Netherlands, has a conventional layout with a city centre surrounded by suburbs. By contrast, Almere, where work began in 1971, was designed as a polynucleated city in which each core is a self-contained entity with its own centre and a distinctive atmosphere and character. The masterplan for Almere, which with a projected population of between 125,000 and 250,000 was to be a substantial 'overflow' town for Amsterdam and the Gooi region, was drawn up by Projectburo Almere. Set up by the IJsselmeerpolders Development Authority to coordinate the planning, this office comprised all the relevant disciplines from urban design and landscape architecture to sociology and economics. In designing the structure of Almere, urban planner T. Koolhaas and landscape architect A. Hosper decided from the outset not to develop the geographical centre of Almere; instead of buildings there is a small lake. Almere-Stad, where construction began in 1979, was the largest core but the first area to be built was the smaller Almere-Haven on the shores of Gooi Lake where work began in 1974. It consists of a town centre, a contemporary echo of an old Zuiderzee village, surrounded by low-rise housing developments. Almere-Haven is the purest and most complete ensemble of 1970s urban design in the Netherlands. Nowhere is there so much small-scale development and variety to be found as here.

During the 1970s the consequences of the 1965 Spatial Planning Act became apparent. The provision allowing municipalities to delay filling in the detail on land use plans until after they had been approved in general outline by the Provincial States, gave rise to the vlekkenplan in which proposed areas of development were indicated as little more than vague splotches on the map. Usually such plans were then developed splotch by splotch which in some cases resulted in planners losing sight of the overall picture. Combined with what was somewhat irreverently referred to 'cauliflower urbanism' (crescents, cul-de-sacs and home zones) it tended to produce a rather diffuse picture, as can be seen in Nieuwegein, which developed as a succession of virtually unrelated neighbourhoods.

The development plan for Houten, a growth area given the task of accommodating 22,000 new inhabitants over 25 years, was drawn up by W. Wissing. It presents a more orderly appearance, not least because of the existing railway line cutting right through the town centre and a motorway girdling the municipality. Situated along this ring road are the new residential areas, facing towards the new centre of Houten which was laid out alongside the former town centre. In the centre around the new railway station there is scant space for the motor car. On 'urban premises' as Wissing called the town centre, 'Shanks's pony, bicycles and mopeds are the modes of transport. The motor car will only be admitted into this picture at a snail's pace'.

The vlekkenplan resulted in one or two instances of uncoordinated urban planning, but on the whole it worked fairly well as a flexible planning instrument capable of accommodating changing conditions. While it may have facilitated the emergence of districts made up of a series of discrete neighbourhoods, this fragmentation was also a reflection of prevailing urban design ideals which were more in sympathy with the smaller scale of the neighbourhood than the large scale of the urban district that had been so popular in the 1960s.

The same concern for the smaller scale was also evident in the cities, where urban renewal was just getting into its stride. The home zone culture penetrated even here. Until the 1960s few had demurred at the way many inner-city areas were turning into dedicated business districts where people worked and shopped but no longer lived. Now, in the 1970s, a backlash against suburbanization led to the idea that the city centre should also be a place where people lived, in particular the less well-off. The culture of the protest generation and the socialist ideal of a more equitable distribution of skills and affluence were particularly evident in the big cities where the tone was usually set by social-democratic politicians. 'Building for the neighbourhood' became the policy here, partly from conviction but also because local residents demanded it. The most celebrated example of such grassroots action were the 'metro riots' in Amsterdam in the early 1970s. Ostensibly directed against the building of the metro, they were first and foremost a protest against the planned demolition and redevelopment of the old working-class Nieuwmarkt area and they eventually resulted in the area being rebuilt on the same scale as before and with a preponderance of low-cost rental housing.

A number of architects played a crucial role in the regeneration of Nieuwmarkt: A. van Eyck, T. Bosch and in their wake P. de Ley, a former associate of Van Eyck. These three had already demonstrated in Zwolle that it was possible to carry out urban renewal in a circumspect manner that respected prior structures.

In the course of the 1970s, this cautious approach to urban renewal made its appearance in all the large and medium-sized Dutch cities with neighbourhoods dating from the turn of the century. In Amsterdam, apart from the inner city, it was applied in the Dapper, Pijp and Kinker neighbourhoods; in The Hague in Schilderswijk and in Rotterdam in Oude Westen and more or less in the shadow of the Shell headquarters on Hofplein, a building described by a Rotterdam alderman as the 'final erection of big business'. The substantial low-rise projects which sprang up here in the 1970s, with their village-like enclaves of affordable housing designed by the architects J. Verhoeven and H. Klunder, were a direct consequence of the belief in the malleable society and the concomitant determination not simply to surrender the inner city to the highest bidder.

Initially, urban planners attempted to introduce new solutions into urban renewal schemes: new subdivisions, new street patterns and new types of dwellings. Not only did these often meet with resistance from local residents, but some innovations, such as new subdivisions, were difficult to implement because of the practice of tackling the neighbourhoods in stages. In most cases, therefore, the planners opted for a form of urban renewal based on the old building lines and eaves heights. Apart from the practical aspect, this approach also had an idealistic component. The existing urban fabric, as it started to be called, was regarded as inherently valuable, a notion that gained increasing currency in the 1980s.

128

J. Verhoeven   housing, Nieuwegein (1976-1980)

J. Verhoeven   Stroveer housing scheme, Rotterdam (1977-1983)

P. de Ley   urban renewal Bickersgracht, Amsterdam (1970-1978)

H. Klunder   housing Haagse Veer, Rotterdam (1977)

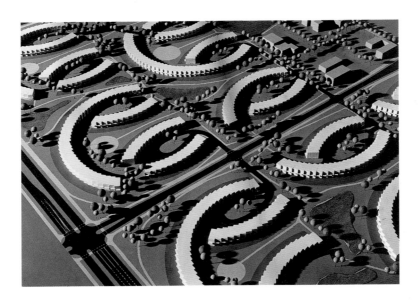

130

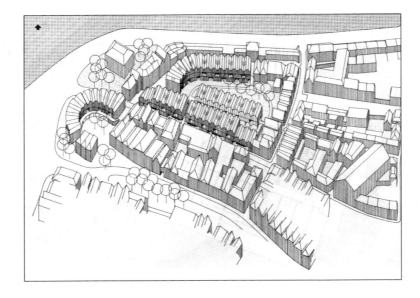

H. Klunder, D. Zuiderhoek   park city, Nieuw Leusden (1969-1972)

Department of Town Planning   design for urban renewal Dapperbuurt, Amsterdam (1971)

A. van Eyck, T.J.J. Bosch   inner-city urban renewal Nieuwstraat and Waterstraat, Zwolle (1975-1977)

132

A. van Eyck, T.J.J. Bosch urban renewal Nieuwmarktbuurt, Amsterdam (1970-1985)

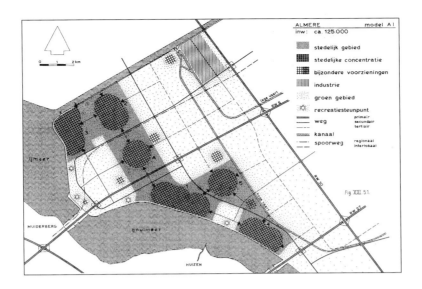

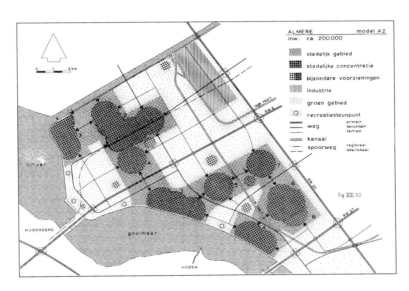

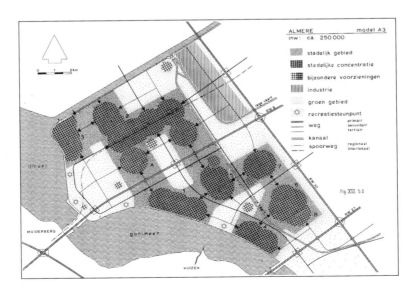

growth models for Almere's polynuclear structure based on various population projections (1970)

134

K. Rijnboutt arcade, Almere-Stad (c. 1985)

D.C. Apon, J.A. van der Berg, A.J. ter Braak, W.B. Tromp development plan for centre,
Almere-Haven (1974-1979)

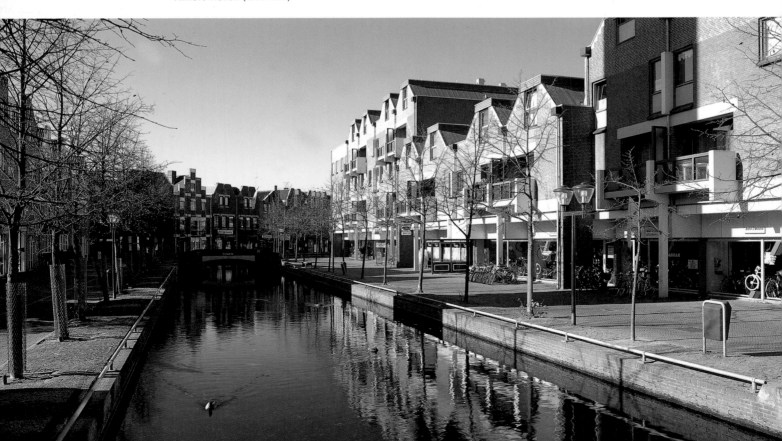

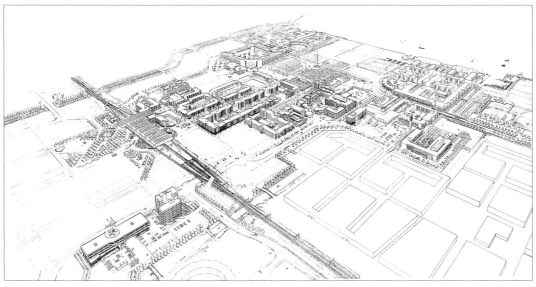

T. Koolhaas, A. Hosper   Almere-Haven, Weerwater and Almere-Stad under construction

IJsselmeerpolders Development Authority   centre Almere-Stad (1979)

1980-1990

The compact city

Around 1980 the city came back into fashion. Whereas in the preceding years the village had been the lodestar of urban design, now it was the metropolis that designers and policymakers looked to as their model in the planning or redevelopment of urban areas. The return of high-rise and the rediscovery of the merits of the perimeter block as spatial planning device are symptomatic of this shift in thinking. After the 'villagey' urbanism of the 1970s, the pendulum swung right through to 'urbane' urbanism. The diffuse vlekkenplan was succeeded by a preference for urbanism with a clear form. Two areas in Amsterdam that were developed in the early 1980s are illustrative of this change: IJ-plein in Amsterdam North, designed by R. Koolhaas and J. Voorberg of OMA, and Venserpolder, between the city and the Bijlmer, realized in accordance with plans drawn up by C. Weeber. Both plans have an exceptionally clear form, that of IJ-plein being based on the principle of open row housing and that of Venserpolder on the perimeter block. The renewed popularity of the perimeter block was not only a question of architectural and urbanist preferences but also reflected the pre-occupation with public safety that dominated society for a while in the 1980s.

The IJ-plein development marks the moment in Dutch urbanism and architecture when modernist history was rediscovered. After analysing a variety of famous examples from the past century that might serve as a model for the subdivision of IJ-plein, the designers opted for a layout consisting of row housing alternating with 'urban villas', compact, medium-rise apartment blocks with two to six, but more usually four units per storey. Weeber's plan for Venserpolder carried with it a plea for an autonomous urban planning discipline. His contention was that urbanism had been diluted in previous decades and absorbed into architecture. As he saw (and sees) it, the quality of public space depends less on the architecture than on the two-dimensional development plan on which it is based. The practical elaboration of this radical thesis in Venserpolder, which received a lot of flak in the professional press, is in almost every respect the antithesis of the home zones of the 1970s: a very simple, uniform layout of austere urban blocks with uninflected facades fronting onto straight streets. The only similarity with the home zone regime is the absence of hierarchy: there is no central point in the district, no square, no distinction between main and secondary roads.

The clear basic form evident in both Venserpolder and IJ-plein runs like a red thread through the urbanism of the 1980s. Among the many plans displaying a clear organization are the masterplans produced by J. Coenen during this decade. In his plan for Vaillantlaan in The Hague the sense of order is achieved mainly through uniform architecture. The KNSM-eiland scheme in the Amsterdam docklands and the redevelopment of the Sphinx Céramique factory site in Maastricht have a formal spatial organization similar to Weeber's Venserpolder. These two projects, designed in the late 1980s and largely realized in the 1990s, possess a strong form and a monumentality that would have been inconceivable in the 1970s.

Strong form was also the guiding principle in the design of new suburban developments. Corpus den Hoorn in Groningen, Nieuw Sloten in Amsterdam and Prinsenland in Rotterdam are all characterized by a high degree of organization. The same is true of Kattenbroek in Amersfoort, designed by A. Bhalotra of Kuiper Compagnons. Here a structure dominated by geometrical forms is combined with an architectural elaboration according to themes. Ranging from the abstract ('autumn') to the fairly concrete ('avenue of courtyards'), these themes were intended to inspire the architects to produce something different from the usual run-of-the-mill architecture. Kattenbroek was only the first of many such examples of thematic urbanism, a trend that derived from a desire for legitimation. In the 1980s the legitimation for designs was usually found in the setting. In no other period was context so important a guide as in this decade. In planning new districts designers strove to relate their designs as much as possible to the existing landscape, even when the latter had been almost completely obliterated by sand fill. In the city, redevelopment and infill projects took their cue from the urban fabric of existing buildings. There was a strong conviction of the importance of spatial continuity and the need to bear witness to the history of the place.

The rediscovery of the city also led to a revival of interest in high-rise. The modest boom in high-rise construction, the results of which were particularly noticeable in the centre of Rotterdam, can be traced to the idea of the compact city. The compact city was a concept that surfaced in the 1980s and with which everyone, from high-rise lobbyists to environmental activists, could agree. A city with a high density and a wide mix of uses was desirable on various counts: it enlivened the city, strengthened the local economy and curbed the growth of mobility.

This view also informed the Fourth Report on Spatial Planning of 1988. Until the 1970s the idea of clustered dispersal had been all the rage but now the government opted for a policy of straightforward concentration. This was so broadly interpreted, however, that more than a dozen cities were designated as 'urban nodes', in effect, centres of new development. The guiding principle of the Fourth Report was that development should take place as much as possible in or close to the cities. At the same time the Green Heart, the agro-industrial area between the Randstad cities, was declared off limits for further development.

The policy of concentration found expression in, among other things, what was usually called urban regeneration. While urban renewal of older neighbourhoods continued as before, a new task had presented itself: the redevelopment of a host of urban sites that had lost their original uses, for the most part former industrial and dockland areas. Plans were drawn up for new residential and work environments, where possible incorporating existing features such as warehouses, factories and quay walls. The largest urban regeneration projects are the Oostelijk Havengebied in Amsterdam, Kop van Zuid in Rotterdam and Sphinx Céramique in Maastricht. Smaller examples are the Zaanoevers in Zaanstad, the station area in Amersfoort and the sites of former textile factories in Almelo. Big or small, the planning process was a long drawn-out affair. The initial impetus for the development of Kop van Zuid, for example, was given in 1981, the year in which the Rotterdam Arts Council held the Architecture International Rotterdam (AIR) festival, for which five foreign designers were invited to give their view of the area's future. This was the first show of public interest in the largely derelict docks area across the river Maas from the city centre. Eventually, in 1987, T. Koolhaas drew up a masterplan for the area which provided for 5,000 dwellings and almost 400,000 m^2 of office space, but it was not until the 1990s that construction reached full swing.

Compared with this, the development of Almere has been highly expeditious. Around 1980, with Almere-Haven nearly finished, construction commenced on Almere-Stad, which was completed in around ten years in accordance with the prevailing principles of clearly structured urban development. The centre is based on an orthogonal system of streets and squares, enclosed by continuous facades. To this classic repertoire of urban forms was added a contemporary version of the nineteenth-century arcade designed by K. Rijnboutt, and one decidedly non-classic element, a dedicated bus lane running right through the town centre. Dedicated bus lanes were a fairly recent strategy for improving public transport reliability and curbing car use. Between 1970 and 1990 the number of cars had doubled from 2.5 million to over 5 million and the number of kilometres travelled had increased from 66 to 136 billion a year (although this actually represented a drop in the rate of growth compared with previous decades).

Suburbanization, which continued unabated in the 1980s despite the renewed interest in the city, was connected with this growth in mobility in two ways. Widespread car ownership made suburbanization possible and, conversely, suburban sprawl stimulated car use. The drift to the suburbs applied not just to housing but also to work, for despite the government's policy of concentration more and more businesses were deserting the city centres. Although this process had been going on for decades, it became particularly noticeable in the 1980s. Business parks were springing up everywhere along feeder roads and motorways. Such locations were eminently accessible for motorists, the offices were relatively cheap to rent and were also visible from the highway, thereby serving as a signboard for the businesses that occupied them. The periphery (a 1980s buzz word) where these business parks were built was often a no man's land in terms of spatial planning. When it came to business parks, municipalities tended to confine themselves to allocating land and providing the bare minimum of infrastructure. Such peripheral zones were usually an uncoordinated mish-mash of wrecker's yards, mobile home encampments, allotments, petrol stations, building materials suppliers and playing fields. Having previously regarded it as not much more than an unkempt wasteland, urban designers now started to discover the charms of such apparently unplanned locations. This was the beginning of a new realism that was to continue into the 1990s whereby urban planners came to accept that even in a country where everything is subject to planning, there will always be some things that they are unable or should not even want to control.

With the rediscovery of the city came renewed interest in public space in the city. The design of the public realm – thanks to celebrated examples in Paris and Barcelona – came to be regarded as a major design task. The design of squares, streets and parks enjoyed a veritable boom during the 1980s. It resulted in an unprecedented quantity of new, specially designed street furniture, pavements and plantings, varying from the blatantly artistic decor designed for Damrak, Rokin and Nieuwmarkt in Amsterdam by the artist A. Schabracq, to A. Hosper's sober refurbishment of the Hague city centre, an exercise in elimination and the removal of visual clutter. That a landscape architect like Hosper should have been awarded the commission to redesign a number streets and squares in The Hague was typical of a 1980s trend in which landscape architects started to abandon their traditional sphere of parks and landscapes. More and more parks were being designed with a minimum of vegetation and it was only a small step from this to the design of squares and other urban public spaces. Nor was it only the landscape architects who invaded the territory of the urban designer; the latter also lost ground to architects, both in the design of the public realm and in the larger development schemes. As such, the upturn experienced by urban design in the 1980s was partly attributable to designers who had had no training in the discipline.

Bureau Bakker & Bleeker, A. Hosper De Kern Gezond project, The Hague (1986)

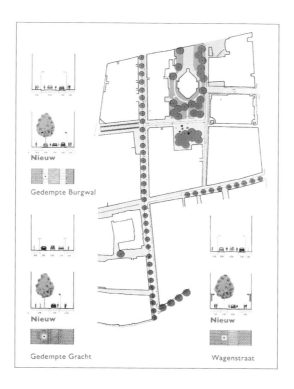

Bureau Bakker & Bleeker, A. Hosper De Kern Gezond project, The Hague (1986)

J. Coenen urban renewal masterplan Vaillantlaan, The Hague (1989-1995)

Benthem Crouwel Architekten, NACO, West 8 Jan Dellaertplein, Schiphol (1988)

Benthem Crouwel Architekten, NACO masterplan, Schiphol (1988)

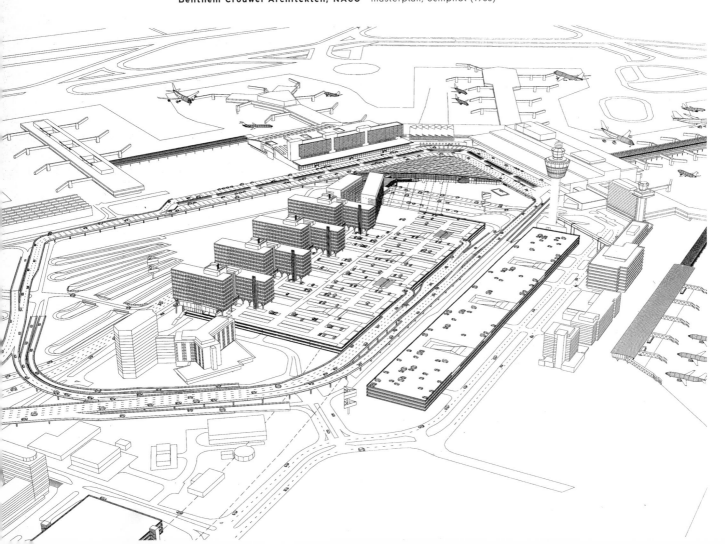

Office for Metropolitan Architecture OMA   masterplan and housing IJ-plein, Amsterdam (1980-1988)

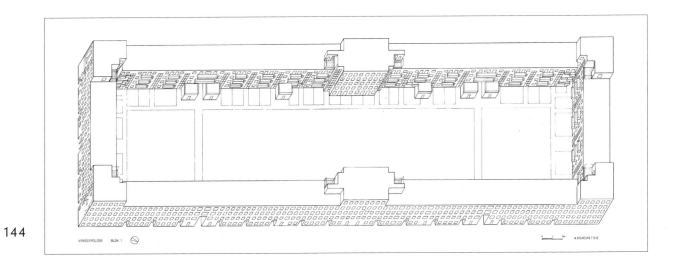

VENSERPOLDER   BLOK 1   AXONOMETRIE

C. Weeber   block 1 Venserpolder, Amsterdam (1982)

C. Weeber   development plan Venserpolder, Amsterdam (1982-1986)

L.L. Lafour and **R. Wijk,** urban design plan with **A. van Eyck, P. de Ley** and **city of Middelburg**
housing Maïsbaai   Middelburg (1987-1991)
T.J.J. Bosch   housing Sijzenbaan, Deventer (1985-1988)

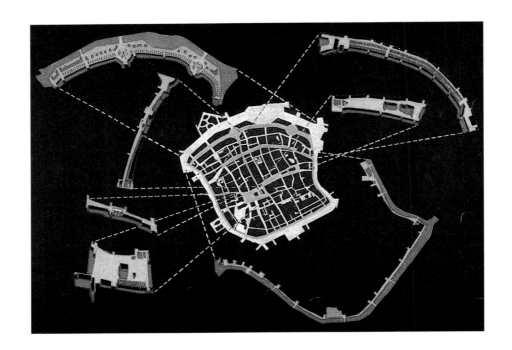

Mecanoo   Space for Space masterplan, Groningen (1989)

J. Coenen   masterplan Sphinx Céramique, Maastricht (1987-)

Mecanoo   Space for Space masterplan, Groningen (1989)

Kuiper Compagnons, A. Bhalotra   masterplan Kattenbroek, Amersfoort (1988-1994)

housing Kattenbroek, Amersfoort (1992)

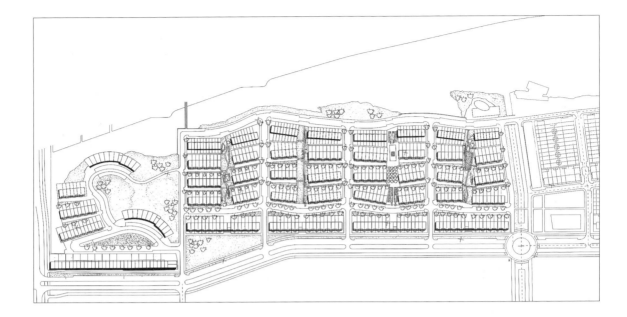

Mecanoo urban design plan Ringvaartplasbuurt Prinsenland, Rotterdam (1988-1993)

F. Palmboom urban design plan Prinsenland, Rotterdam (1988-1993)

Mecanoo   urban design plan and housing Ringvaartplasbuurt Prinsenland, Rotterdam (1988-1993)

Weena high-rise, Rotterdam (situation 1992)

153

A. Rossi AIR competition design Kop van Zuid, Rotterdam (1982)

T. Koolhaas Associates urban design plan Kop van Zuid, Rotterdam (1987-)

1990-2000

New expansion districts

In 1990 a supplement to the Fourth Report on Spatial Planning **was published:** the Fourth Report Extra. **Its Dutch acronym VINEX was the most frequently used word in Dutch urbanism during the last decade of the twentieth century. There is scarcely an urban area in the Netherlands without one or more VINEX sites. These are locations earmarked for development within the framework of the Fourth Report Extra, usually as residential areas, sometimes in combination with work and recreation. What had previously been known simply as expansion districts were now suddenly called VINEX districts. The VINEX building pro- gramme, which originally envisaged the construction of around one million houses by the year 2005, was revised downwards to 600,000 plus at the end of the decade. Construction of the VINEX districts commenced in the mid-1990s.**

Leidsche Rijn, a new urban quarter between Utrecht and Vleuten-De Meern, is with 30,000 dwellings the largest VINEX scheme. The masterplan drawn up for the area by the Max. 1 architectural office was intentionally flexible: by not laying down in advance precisely how Leidsche Rijn should look, it allowed room for adjustments until quite late in the planning process. The plan is based on a concept of urbanism in which the 'orgware', as Max. 1 calls it, is seen as the determining factor. 'Orgware' encompasses all the administrative and political factors which together make up a 'topography of possibilities and restrictions' that has a formative influence on any urban design plan. This emphasis on external conditions deviated from the interpretation of urbanism that had been current since the 1980s in which roads, watercourses, specific building types and key landscape elements were the main points of reference. Sometimes the orgware was supplemented by a second layer consisting of thematized plans and elements. The themes might be metaphorical (a frequent post-Kattenbroek occurrence) but more usually they were in the nature of guidelines regarding the type of dwelling, the materials to be used, the ordering of the facade, the design of public space and the types of trees and shrubs to be planted. In K. Christiaanse's spatial masterplan for the GWL site in Amsterdam, for example, the shape of the housing blocks and the colour of the brick were determined in advance. In similar fashion, West 8 in its spatial masterplan for the Borneo-Sporenburg district in Amsterdam specified the type of dwelling the architects were to design.

This approach to urbanism, in which the designer details precisely how the buildings, paving and planting should look, can be found in many of the residential areas built during the 1990s. The idea was to give each district and each neighbourhood a distinct identity of its own. In practice, spatial and architectural variations in VINEX areas were circumscribed by the slim financial margins obtaining in a market no longer dictated by the government but by commerce.

While the VINEX districts were springing up on the outskirts of cities everywhere, the city centres themselves were undergoing radical redevelopment. In Rotterdam a large part of the city centre was completely transformed by a series of development projects. The construction of a railway tunnel under the river Maas led to the demolition of a distinctive but now obsolete railway viaduct. Part of the vacated land was redesigned by West 8, the office that was also responsible for the city's revamped Schouwburgplein. Beursplein, a post-war reconstruction ensemble, became the Beurstraverse, a sunken shopping mall designed by the American firm, The Jerde Partnership. Similar developments occurred in the post-war city centres of Nijmegen (designed by Soeters Van Eldonk) and Hengelo (Bolles & Wilson). In The Hague the Utrechtse Baan was built over in several places during the 1990s while the area between Spui and Central Station underwent a complete metamorphosis. Apart from R. Meier's city hall, the most striking element here is The Resident, a residential/work complex designed by the Luxembourg urban designer and leading proponent of the compact city, R. Krier. It is a traditional piece of urban fabric with a baroque-style square as centrepiece. In Utrecht, as part of the Utrecht Centre Project (UCP), work began on the redevelopment of Hoog Catharijne, the train and bus stations and the Jaarbeurs exhibition complex. Major station precinct conversions were also carried out in other cities including Arnhem and Rotterdam.

All these projects can be construed as amendments to post-war urban design. Indeed, such schemes, which entailed the reversal of earlier interventions, were often described in terms of repairing the city. Spatial reparation was not an end in itself, however. In most cases the prime motivation was economic. The attractiveness of the built environment was only one aspect of a process aimed at revitalizing the inner city. Attracting and retaining a full complement of shops, businesses, restaurants and bars, cultural facilities and housing was seen as a sure way of keeping the economy of a city turning. Such schemes were often characterized by lofty ambitions. Sometimes too lofty, as in the spectacular design produced for the banks of the IJ inlet in Amsterdam by a group of designers headed by R. Koolhaas's OMA. Politicians and potential investors rejected the plan as too risky. Work on another big OMA masterplan began shortly before the turn of century: the radical transformation of the centre of Almere-Stad which only ten years after completion was felt to be in need of a metamorphosis.

Such processes of amendment were not confined to city centres but also took place in many post-war suburbs. The demolition of some of the high-rise apartment blocks in Amsterdam's Bijlmer and their replacement by a contemporary, low-rise development lacking the previous strict separation of slow and fast traffic is the most remarkable. Another striking example can be seen in the 1950s Slotermeer district in Amsterdam West, part of C. van Eesteren's General Extension Plan (AUP) of 1934. The Noorderhof neighbourhood built here to a design by Krier breaks with the open structure of the AUP. Instances of this new traditionalism can also be found in many of the VINEX districts. Although dominated by the contemporary repertoire, they also contain elements in which the principles of the garden city are combined with an architecture reminiscent of the restrained style that was popular for villas in the 1930s.

The changes wrought in housing estates built in the 1950s and 1960s were part of a second wave of urban renewal. Scarcely had the first round of classic urban renewal in districts from the prewar period been completed in the early 1990s, than a new task presented itself in the form of the post-war districts. The cautious respect shown to the prewar urban areas was seldom evident in this second round of urban renewal. Neighbourhoods with open row housing were often dealt with rather heavy-handedly. Apart from demolition and radical remodelling, this manifested itself in the building over of the abundant open space.

The spate of big projects in the city centres and on the urban outskirts all display enormous get-up-and-go vigour. At first glance the same might seem to be true of the mega-projects that have been the focus of so much political and

public interest in the 1990s, such as the high speed train links with Belgium and Germany, the Betuwe freight line to Germany and the expansion of Schiphol Airport or its relocation (to an off-shore site in the North Sea, for example), and of the project to record the country's ecological main structure, a continuum of valuable natural environments. The truth is, however, that such large-scale schemes are seldom executed with alacrity in the Netherlands. With the exception of the strengthening of the river embankments in the wake of two successive near-floods in the mid-1990s, big projects are characterized by a seemingly interminable genesis for which the word 'vigour' would be quite inappropriate. It is customary for the initial presentation of a proposal to be followed by a long-drawn-out period involving one or more rounds of political decision-making, consultation, Environmental Impact Reports and legal proceedings instituted by the plan's opponents. The result of all this, to take just one example, is that the Netherlands, unlike its neighbours, had still not built a single metre of the high speed line by the year 2000. But as well as its many obvious disadvantages, the slowness of the Dutch consultative culture also has its bright side: major blunders in the field of spatial planning are rare.

Whereas in the decades immediately after the war it was confidently believed that a national spatial planning policy would be capable of managing any and all developments within national borders, by century's end this idea had vanished for good. Highly revealing in this respect is the New Map of the Netherlands, an initiative of J. Schrijnen of the Association of Dutch Urban Designers (BNS), which incorporates all the proposed spatial transformations on Dutch soil up to the year 2010. The mere fact that such a map did not yet exist, indicates that no one in the Netherlands, not even the national government, had any clear picture of what was going on.

Projects like the New Map of the Netherlands are typical of the period of reflection in which the urban design discipline found itself at the end of the twentieth century. Practitioners were interested not just in the question of where precisely Dutch urbanism stood, but also in the hypothetical question 'what if?'. For instance, in the context of another AIR event, this time focusing on the Alexanderpolder, OMA analysed how full (or empty) the Netherlands would look if all its sixteen million inhabitants were to be housed in a city with the density of New York or Los Angeles. A variation on this was MVRDV's project involving the hypothetical city of Metacity/Datatown which the practice used to investigate what happens in a self-supporting city, four hundred square kilometres in area and with a density four times as high as that in the Netherlands. Another plan by MVRDV invoked the hypothetical situation of the province of North Brabant as one big urban area with one function per municipality. Of a similar order is the map of the Randstad produced by the Schie 2.0 practice in which the conurbation appears as one gigantic metropolis. One component of this map, the rail connections, is rendered in the style of the maps of the London Underground or the Paris Métro.

These hypothetical proposals may at first glance seem rather gratuitous but this is not necessarily the case. They may also be read as strategies for setting ideas about the design of the Netherlands on a different track, for breaking away from fixed assumptions and looking at urbanism and spatial planning in a different way. For urban design, which evolved into an independent discipline during the twentieth century, and which is now professionalized and institutionalized, such forms of reflection may be seen as a sign of maturity.

Office for Metropolitan Architecture OMA   city centre masterplan, Almere-Stad (1994/1995-)

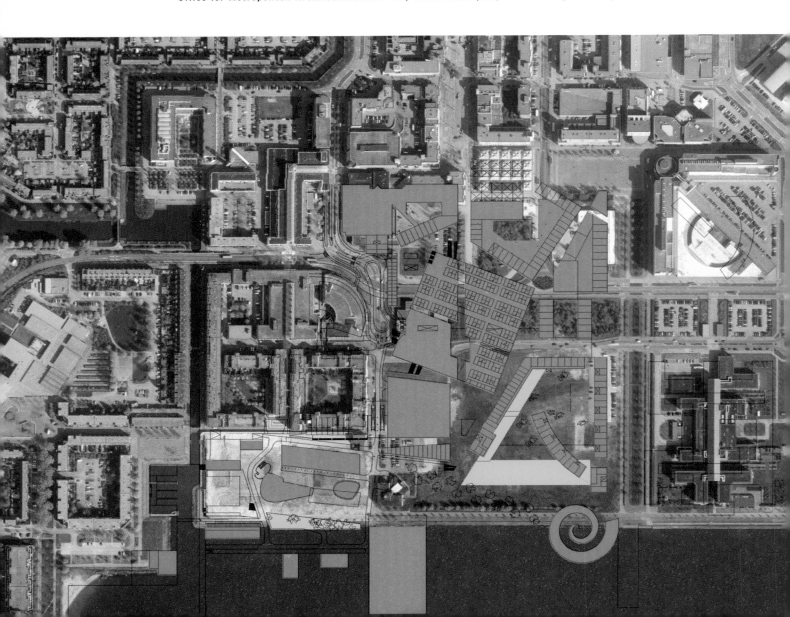

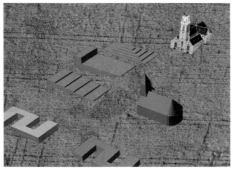
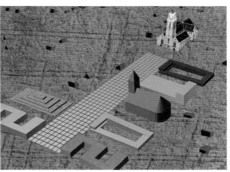

MVRDV   urban design study Rotterdam 2045 (1995)

Projectbureau Kop van Zuid   Kop van Zuid, Rotterdam (1991)

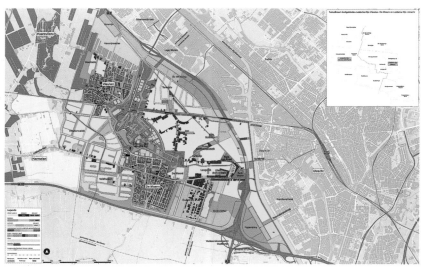

Max. 1 maquette urban design plan Leidsche Rijn, Utrecht (1993-)

Projectbureau Leidsche Rijn, city of Utrecht urban design plan Leidsche Rijn, Utrecht (master map 1999)

UCP computer simulation future situation Utrecht Centrum Project (UCP), Utrecht (1997-)

Rijnsweerd business park, Utrecht (situation 1998)

162

S. Soeters development plan Java Island, Eastern docks area Amsterdam (1989-)

Urban district Geuzenveld/Slotermeer, P. Boekschooten, R. Krier development plan Noorderhof,
Amsterdam West (1995-1999)

West 8   development plan Borneo Sporenburg, Eastern docks area Amsterdam (1994-)

J. Coenen   development plan KNSM island, Eastern docks area Amsterdam (1989-)

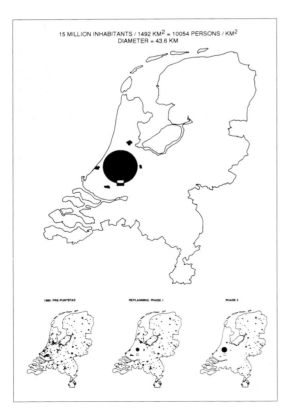

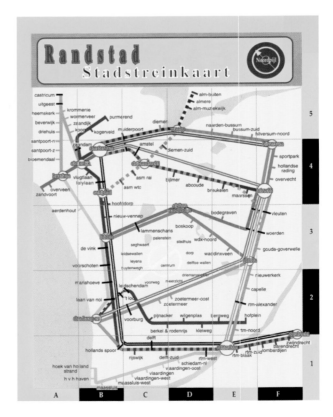

Office for Metropolitan Architecture OMA, K. Christiaanse   Dedemsvaartweg housing festival, The Hague (1988)

Office for Metropolitan Architecture OMA   concentrated development in the Green Heart, Puntstad (1993)

Schie 2.0, L. Verwey   map of Randstad intercity train network (1996)

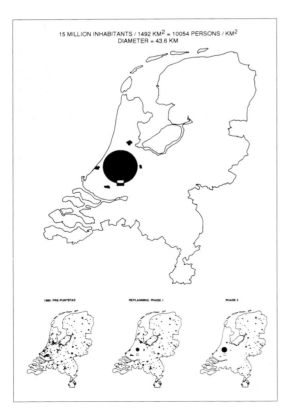
15 MILLION INHABITANTS / 1492 KM² = 10054 PERSONS / KM²
DIAMETER = 43.6 KM

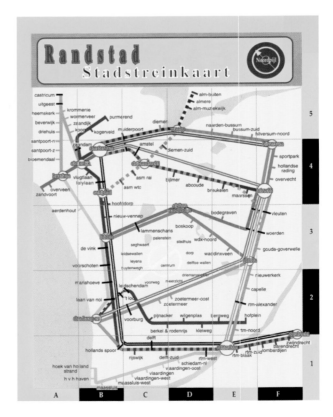

MVRDV North-Brabant 2050 (1999)

W.T.H. Ellerman, A.H. Veerbeek   development plan and housing Park Veursehout, Leidschendam (1995-1999)

R. Krier, S. Soeters masterplan The Resident, The Hague (1988-)

K. Christiaanse, Architects & Planners development plan GWL site, Amsterdam (1993-1998)

West 8 Carrascoplein, Amsterdam (1992-1998)

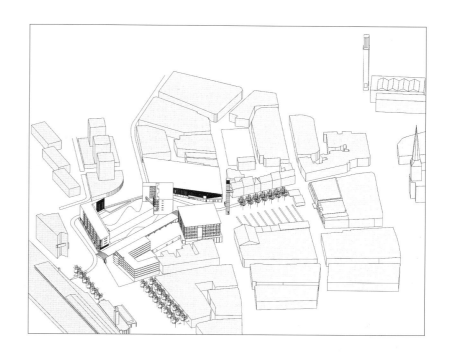

J.B. Bolles & P. Wilson redevelopment plan for De Brink housing/shopping complex,
Hengelo (1998-1999)
West 8 Carrascoplein, Amsterdam (1992-1998)

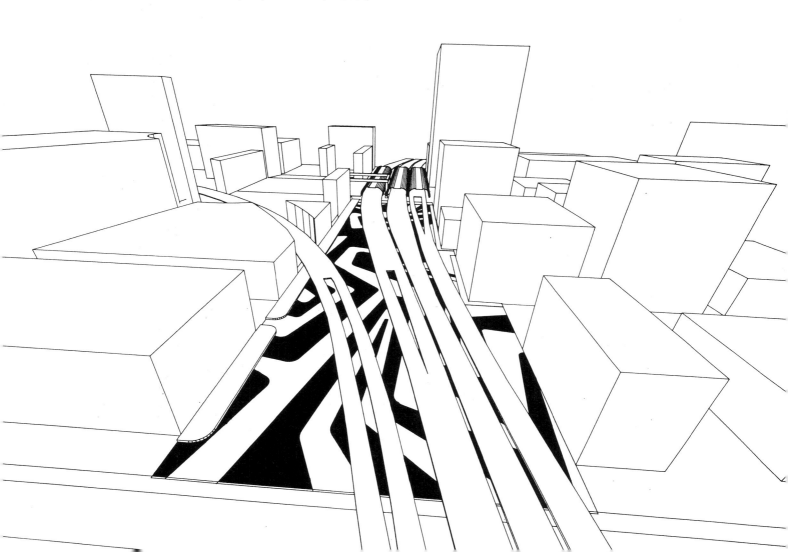

170

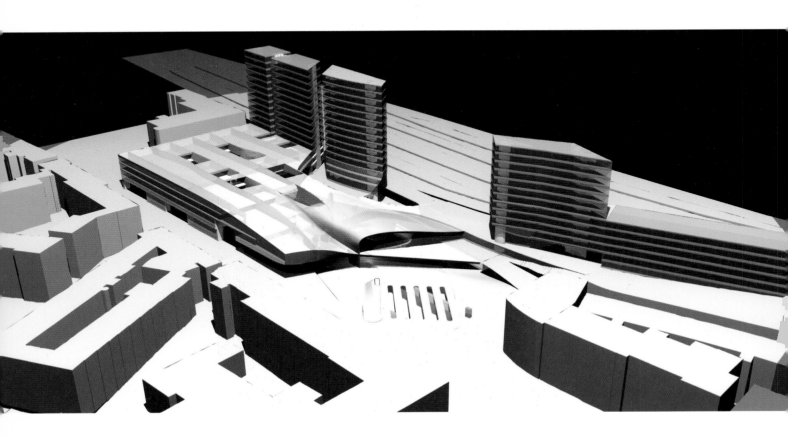

MVRDV   Flight Forum business location, Airport Eindhoven (1998)

UN Studio   masterplan station precinct, Arnhem (1996-)

de Architekten cie./Pi de Bruijn with Spatial Planning Agency   masterplan South Axis and High Speed
Train terminal WTC, Amsterdam (proposal 1999)

de Architekten cie./Pi de Bruijn with S.P. van Breda, The Jerde Partnership   Beurstraverse shopping
centre, Rotterdam (1991-1996)

Bibliography

1900-1910

Berlage, H.P., **Beschouwingen over bouwkunst en hare ontwikkeling** (Rotterdam, 1911)

Berlage, H.P., 'Stedenbouw I', **De beweging. Algemeen Maandtijdschrift voor Letteren, Kunst, Wetenschap en Staatkunde** 10 (1941-1), 'Stedenbouw II en III', **idem** (1914-2)

Bruinwold Riedel, J., **Tuinsteden** (Utrecht, 1906)

Fockema, S.J., 'The Garden City Idea in The Netherlands Before 1930', **Stedebouw & Volkshuisvesting** 44 (1963), p.95-107

Fockema Andreae, J.P., **De hedendaagsche stedenbouw** (Utrecht, 1912)

Haan, J. de, **Villaparken in Nederland. Een onderzoek aan de hand van het villapark Duin en Daal te Bloemendaal 1897-1940** (Haarlem, 1986)

Haan, J. de, **Gooise villaparken. Ontwikkeling van het buitenwonen in het Gooi tussen 1874 en 1940** (Haarlem, 1990)

Jansen, J.C.G.M., **Architectuur en stedebouw in Limburg 1850-1940** (Zwolle/Zeist, 1994)

Polano, S., **Hendrik Petrus Berlage. Het complete werk** (Alphen a/d Rijn, 1988) English edition: **Hendrik Petrus Berlage. Complete works** (New York, 1987)

Sociaal-technische Vereeniging van demokratische ingenieurs en architecten, **Prijsvraag voor het ontwerpen van een tuinstad-wijk. Jury-rapport met reproducties der beste ontwerpen** (Amsterdam, 1915)

1910-1920

Berlage, H.P., A. Keppler, W. Kromhout and J. Wils, **Arbeiderswoningen in Nederland** (Rotterdam, 1921)

Fraenkel, F.F., **Het plan Amsterdam-Zuid van H.P. Berlage** (Alphen a/d Rijn, 1976) English summary

Gaillard, K. and B. Dokter (eds.), **Berlage en Amsterdam Zuid** (Amsterdam/Rotterdam, 1992)

Hoeven, E. van der, **J.J.P. Oud en Bruno Taut. Ontwerpen voor een nieuwe stad: Rotterdam-Berlijn** (Rotterdam, 1994)

Kruiger, J.B.T., **Architectuur en stedebouw in Drenthe 1850-1940** (Zwolle/Zeist, 1991)

Kuiper, J.A., **Visueel en dynamisch. De stedebouw van Granpré Molière en Verhagen 1915-1950** (Delft, 1991)

Lamberts, B., H. Middag, **Architectuur en stedebouw in Overijssel 1850-1940** (Zwolle/Zeist, 1991)

1920-1930

Bergeijk, H. van, **Willem Marinus Dudok. Architect-stedebouwkundige 1884-1974** (Naarden, 1995)

Bock, M. et al., **Van het Nieuwe Bouwen naar een Nieuwe Architectuur. Groep '32: Ontwerpen, gebouwen, stedebouwkundige plannen 1925-1945** (Den Haag, 1983)

Bosma, K. (ed.), **Het Nieuwe Bouwen. Amsterdam 1920-1960** (Delft/Amsterdam, 1983) Dutch/English

Casseres, J.M. de, **Stedebouw** (Amsterdam, 1926)

Casseres, J.M. de, **Grondslagen der Planologie** (Amsterdam, 1933)

Duiker, J.B., **Hoogbouw** (Rotterdam/Brussel, 1930)

Ottenhof, F. (ed.), **Goedkoope arbeiderswoningen (1936)** (Amsterdam, 1981)

Rossem, V. van, **C. van Eesteren. Het idee van de functionele stad. Een lezing met lichtbeelden 1928/C. van Eesteren. The idea of the functional city. A lecture with slides 1928** (Rotterdam/Den Haag, 1997) Dutch/English

Witteveen, W.G., **Het uitbreidingsplan voor het Land van Hoboken** (Haarlem, 1927)

1930-1940

De 8 en Opbouw, **De organische woonwijk in open bebouwing** (Amsterdam, 1932)

Algemeen Uitbreidingsplan van Amsterdam. Grondslagen voor de stedebouwkundige ontwikkeling van Amsterdam; deel 1: Nota van toelichtingen, deel 2: Bijlagen (Amsterdam, 1935)

Blijstra, R., **C. van Eesteren** (Amsterdam, 1971)

Boschplan. Rapport van de commissie voor het Boschplan Amsterdam (Amsterdam, 1931)

Bosma, K., 'Ideeën over wederopbouw. P. Verhagen en de stedebouw', **Plan** 1984, nr. 3, p.35-41

Bosma, K. (ed.), **Architectuur en stedebouw in oorlogstijd. De wederopbouw van Middelburg, 1940-1948** (Rotterdam, 1988)

Bremer, J. and H. Reedijk, **Bouwen '20-'40. De Nederlandse bijdrage aan het nieuwe bouwen** (Eindhoven, 1971)

Embden, S.J. van, **Amsterdam's toekomstige gedaante** (Amsterdam/Münster, 1931)

Geest, J. van, **J.J. van Emben** (Rotterdam, 1996) English summary

Geest, J. van and K. Schipper, **Jos Klijnen** (Rotterdam, 1999) English summary

Hellinga, H. et al., **Algemeen Uitbreidingsplan Amsterdam 50 jaar: 1935-1985** (Amsterdam, 1985)

Liesbrock, H. and S. Blumberger (eds.), **Die neue Stadt: Rotterdam im 20.Jahrhundert, Utopie und Realität** (Münster, 1993)

Merkelbach, B., 'Woonwijken', **de 8 en Opbouw** jrg.3 (1932) 13, p.123-130

Rossem, V. van, **Het Algemeen Uitbreidingsplan van Amsterdam. Geschiedenis en ontwerp Cornelis van Eesteren, architect urbanist, deel 2** (Rotterdam, 1993)

Wils, J., **De sierende elementen van de bouwkunst** (Rotterdam/Brussel, 1923)

1940-1950

Bijhouwer, J.T.P., **De wijkgedachte** (Wageningen, 1947)

Bock, M. et al., **Van het Nieuwe Bouwen naar een Nieuwe Architectuur. Groep '32: ontwerpen, gebouwen, stedebouwkundige plannen 1925-1945** (Den Haag, 1983)

Bosma, K. and C. Wagenaar (eds.), **Een geruisloze doorbraak. De geschiedenis van architectuur en stedebouw tijdens de bezetting en de wederopbouw van Nederland** (Rotterdam, 1995)

Eesteren, C. van, **De conceptie van onze hedendaagse nederzettingen en cultuurlandschappen, hun verschijningsvormen en uitdrukking** (Amsterdam, 1948)

Embden, S.J. van, **De Streek-stad, de stad der toekomst. Aantekeningen over de toekomst van de Nederlandse stedebouw** (Amsterdam, 1948)

Granpré Molière, M.J., **Woorden en werken van Granpré Molière** (Heemstede, 1953)

Granpré Molière, M.J., **Stedebouw** (z.p., z.j.)

Idsinga, T. and J. Schilt, **Architect W. van Tijen 1894-1974** (Den Haag, 1987)

Lohuizen, Th.K. van, **Een eenheid van het stedebouwkundig werk** (Rotterdam, 1948)

Pet, J.C.L.B., 'Romantiek in de stedebouw', **Forum** jrg.3 (1948) 5, p.117-120

Ravesteyn, L.J.C.J. van, **Rotterdam in de twintigste eeuw. De ontwikkeling van de stad vóór 1940** (Rotterdam, 1948)

Stam-Beese, C.I.A., 'Stedebouwkundige studie', **Forum** jrg.4 (1949) 2/3, p.70-71

Wagenaar, C., **Welvaartsstad in wording: de wederopbouw van Rotterdam, 1940-1952** (Rotterdam, 1992) English summary

Wils, J., **Overheidsbemoeienis met stedebouw: een blik in de toekomst** (Leiden, 1940)

Zanstra, P. et al., **Bouwen, van woning tot stad. Eenige aspecten van den stedebouw, het woningbedrijf, de woningarchitectuur en de technische voorzieningen van de woningen, alsmede van verschillende daarmee samenhangende onderwerpen** (Amsterdam, 1946)

1950-1960

Bakema, J.B., **Woning en woonomgeving (8 voordrachten over de ontwikkeling van woningbouw en stedebouw 1930-1975)** (Delft, 1977)

Broek, J.H. van der (ed.), **Prospectus. Proeve van uitvoering** (Amsterdam/Rotterdam/Brussel, 1957)

Dissel, A.M.C., **59 jaar eigengereide doeners in Flevoland, Noordoostpolder en Wieringermeer. Rijksdienst voor de IJsselmeerpolders 1930-1989** (Zutphen, 1991) English summary

Heinemeijer, W.F., **Vijftig jaar actief achter de Afsluitdijk** (Zutphen, 1986)

Hemel, Z., **Het landschap van de IJsselmeerpolders. Planning, inrichting en vormgeving. Cornelis van Eesteren, architect urbanist, deel 4** (Rotterdam, 1994)

'De Noord-Oostpolder', **Forum** (1955) 1-2 (with texts by a.o. J.T.P. Bijhouwer and M.J. Granpré Molière)

Stuvel, H.J., **Het Deltaplan. De geboorte** (Amsterdam, 1956)

1960-1970

Bakema, J.B., **Van stoel tot stad. Een verhaal over mensen en ruimte** (Zeist, 1964)

Bakema, J.B. and J.H. van den Broek, **Stad op Pampus. Studie van een lineaire stad in recreatiegebied** (Rotterdam, 1965)

Barbieri, S.U. et al., **Stedebouw in Rotterdam. Plannen en opstellen 1940-1981** (Amsterdam, 1981)

Bolte, W. and J. Meijer, **Van Berlage tot Bijlmer. Architectuur en stedelijke politiek** (Nijmegen, 1981)

Buiter, H., **Hoog Catharijne. De wording van het winkelhart van Nederland** (Utrecht, 1993)

Eyck, A. van, Th. Bosch, P. de Ley and G. Knemeijer, **Wonen in de binnenstad van Zwolle** (Zwolle, z.j.)

Geurts, A.J., **Lelystad, Stedebouwkundige ontwikkeling en vormgeving** (Lelystad, 1995)

Sluijs, F. van der, **Haagse Stedebouw, mijn ervaringen in de jaren 1946-1983** (Utrecht, 1989)

Velzen, E. van, 'De parallelle stad. Aspecten van het stedebouwkundig werk van Aldo van Eyck', **Oase** 1990 nr. 26/27, p.46-63

1970-1980

Buro Prof. Jo Coenen, **De sphinx ontrafeld. Planbeschrijving Sphinx Ceramique terrein Maastricht** (Eindhoven, 1988)

Brouwer P., **Van stad naar stedelijkheid. Planning en planconceptie van Lelystad en Almere 1959-1974** (Rotterdam, 1997)

Derde Nota over de Ruimtelijke Ordening, deel 1: Oriënteringsnota Ruimtelijke Ordening (1973), deel 2: Verstedelijkingsnota. Beleidsvoornemens over Spreiding, Verstedelijking en Mobiliteit (1976), deel 3: Nota Landelijke Gebieden (1977), deel 3a: Beleidsvoornemens over Ontwikkeling, Inrichting en Beheer (1977) (Den Haag, 1983)

Huygen, P., **Emmen. De bouw van een aangename stad in het groen** (Rotterdam 1995)

Koolhaas, R., **Delirious New York. A Retroactive Manifesto for Manhattan** (Rotterdam, 1978/1994) English

Tromp, C., 'Van vlekkenplan tot Nieuwegein', **Vrij Nederland** 27 augustus 1988

Voet, D., **Emmen: een modelstad op menselijke maat. Opvattingen over de stedebouw 1950-1980** (Rotterdam, 1992)

Vroom, M.J. and J.H.A. Meeus, **Learning from Rotterdam. Investigating the process of urban park design, layout and management of public open space in Rotterdam** (Londen/New York, 1990) English

Woord en Beeld Mediaprojecten, Den Haag (ed.), **Nota de Kern gezond. Plan voor de herinrichting van de openbare ruimte in de Haagse binnenstad** (Den Haag, z.j.)

1980-1990

Amsterdam Waterfront, **Ondernemingsplan ontwikkeling IJ-oevers Amsterdam** (Amsterdam, 1993)

De Architectuur van de Ruimte. Nota over het Architectuurbeleid 1997-2000 (Den Haag, 1996)

Bekaert, G. et al., **Verkenningen in de ruimte. Vijf beschouwingen over Stad Beeld Eindhoven** Eindhoven, 1991)

Bout, J. van den and E. Pasveer (eds.), **Kop van Zuid** (Rotterdam, 1994) Dutch/English

Frieling, D.H., **Wij eisen geluk** (Delft, 1997) (M. Kloos in gesprek met prof. ir. D.H. Frieling over de Bijlmermeer)

Gemeente Maastricht/Dienst stadsontwikkeling, **Structuurvisie Maastricht 1990-2000. Stad in evenwicht, balans in beweging** (Maastricht, 1989)

1990-2000

Gemeente Maastricht, **Rivieroevers Maastricht. Ruimtelijk scharnier van twee stadsdelen** (Maastricht, 1992)

Geuze, A. and West 8, **In Holland staat een huis** (Rotterdam, 1995)

Harseman, H., R. Bijhouwer and S. Cusveller et al. (eds.), **Landschapsarchitectuur en stedebouw in Nederland 93-95/Landscape architecture and town planning in the Netherlands 93-95** (Bussum, 1996) Dutch/English

Harseman, H., R. Bijhouwer and S. Cusveller et al. (eds.), **Landschapsarchitectuur en stedebouw in Nederland 95-97/Landscape architecture and town planning in the Netherlands 95-97** (Bussum, 1998) Dutch/English

Hoog, C.M., R.F.C. Stroink and P.W. Spangenberg, **Stedebouw in de jaren '80. 10 plananalyses, studierapport 37 Rijksplanologische Dienst** (Den Haag, 1987)

Koolhaas, R., **S,M,L,XL** (Rotterdam, 1995) English

Metz, T. and M. Pflug, **De nieuwe kaart van Nederland. Atlas van Nederland in 2005** (Rotterdam, 1997)

MVRDV, **FARMAX. Excursions on Density** (Rotterdam, 1998) English

MVRDV, **Metacity. Data Town** (Rotterdam, 1999) English

Nationaal Milieubeleidsplan, Tweede Kamer 1988-1989, 21137, nrs. 1-2 (Den Haag, 1989)

Natuurbeleidsplan, regeringsbeslissing, Tweede Kamer 1989-1990, 21149 (Den Haag, 1990)

De periferie centraal. Inspiratie en ambities bij de ontwikkeling van perifere VINEX-lokaties (Rotterdam, 1994)

Ravesteijn, A. et al., **Jo Coenen en de Vaillantlaan. Een nieuwe visie op stedebouw en stadsvernieuwing** (Rotterdam, 1996) English summary

Regionaal Structuurplan 1995-2005 (Amsterdam, 1995)

Rossem, V. van, **Stadbouwkunst: de stedelijke ruimte als architectonische opgave. Rob Krier in Den Haag: de Resident** (Rotterdam, 1996) English edition: **Civil Art: Urban Space as Architectural Task. Rob Krier in The Hague: the Resident**

Tellinga, J. (ed.), **Op Europees spoor. De Nederlandse aansluiting op het netwerk van de hogesnelheidslijn** (Rotterdam, 1999)

Vreeze, N. (ed.), **De periferie centraal. Inspiraties en ambities bij de ontwikkeling van perifere VINEX-lokaties** (Rotterdam, 1994)

VROM, **De Ruimte van Nederland Startnota Ruimtelijke Ordening 1999** (Den Haag, 1999)

Wallis de Vries, G. and R. Borgonjen, **Kattenbroek. Groeistad Amersfoort en Ashok Bhalotra** (Rotterdam, 1997) English summary

General

d'Ancona, H., C. Boekraad, G. Brinkgreve et al., **Nederlandse architectuur en stedebouw '45-'80** (Amsterdam, 1984)

Baaij, H. (ed.), **Rotterdam 650 jaar. Vijftig jaar wederopbouw** (Utrecht, 1990)

Bakker, M.M. and F.M. van de Poll, **Architectuur en stedebouw in Amsterdam 1850-1940** (Zwolle/Zeist, 1992)

Baljon, L. et al., **Expeditie L.A.** (Rotterdam, 1995)

Barbieri, S.U. (ed.), **Architectuur en planning. Nederland 1940-1980** (Rotterdam, 1983)

Barbieri, S.U. (ed.), **De Kop van Zuid. Ontwerp en onderzoek** (Rotterdam, 1982)

Beek, J. van der, **Architectuurgids Groningen 1900-1990** (Groningen, 1990)

Beekman, P., **Eindhoven stadsontwikkeling 1900-1960** (Mierlo, 1982)

Bekkering, H.C., **Voetlicht op het stedebouwkundig ontwerpen in het Fin de siècle. Naar een stedebouw van conventie** (Delft, 1999)

Blijstra, R., **2000 jaar Utrecht. Stedebouwkundige ontwikkeling van castrum tot centrum** (Utrecht/Antwerpen, 1969)

Blijstra, R., **Nederlandse stedebouw na 1900** (Amsterdam, z.j.) English edition: **Town-planning in the Netherlands since 1900**

Boekraad, C. (ed.), **Van ruimte tot rizoom. Standpunten in de Nederlandse architectuur** (Rotterdam, 1994)

Boelens, L., **Stedebouw en planologie. Een onvoltooid project. Naar het communicatief handelen in de ruimtelijke planning en ontwerppraktijk** (Delft, 1990)

Boer, N. de, **De Randstad bestaat niet. De onmacht tot grootstedelijk beleid** (Rotterdam, 1996)

Boer, N. de and D. Lambert, **Woonwijken. Nederlandse stedenbouw 1945-1985** (Rotterdam, 1987)

Boomkens, R., **Ontwerpen voor de onmogelijke stad** (Amsterdam, 1993)

Boomkens, R., **Een drempelwereld. Moderne ervaring en stedelijke openbaarheid** (Rotterdam, 1998) English summary

Bosch, A. and W. van der Han, **Twee eeuwen Rijkswaterstaat 1798-1998** (Zaltbommel, 1998)

Bosma, K. et al. (eds.), **Het Nieuwe Bouwen Amsterdam 1920-1960** (Delft/Amsterdam, 1983) Dutch/English

Bosma, K. and H. Hellinga (eds.), **De regie van de stad. Noord-Europese stedebouw 1900-2000** (Rotterdam, 1997) English edition: **Mastering the City. North-European City Planning 1900-2000**

Bosma, K. and C. Wagenaar (eds.), **Een geruisloze doorbraak: de geschiedenis van architectuur en stedebouw tijdens de bezetting en de wederopbouw van Nederland** (Rotterdam, 1995)

Bosma, K., **Ruimte voor een nieuwe tijd. Vormgeving van de Nederlandse regio 1900-1950** (Rotterdam, 1993)

Bruin, W. de (ed.), **VOL. Het debat over de ruimtelijke inrichting van Nederland** (Amsterdam/de Volkskrant, 1997)

Buch, J., **Een eeuw Nederlandse architectuur 1880-1990** (Rotterdam, 1993) English edition: **A Century of Architecture in the Netherlands 1880-1990**

Cammen, H. van der (ed.), **Nieuw Nederland 2050. Onderwerp van ontwerp; deel 1: achtergronden, deel 2: beeldverhalen** (Den Haag, 1987)

Cammen, H. van der and L.A. de Klerk, **Ruimtelijke Ordening, van plannen komen plannen** (Utrecht/Amsterdam, 1986)

Cammen, H. van der (ed.), **Four Metropolises in Western Europe. Development and urban planning of London, Paris, Randstad Holland and the Ruhr region** (Assen/Maastricht, 1988) English

Camp, D' L. and M. Provoost (eds.), **Stadstimmeren. 650 jaar Rotterdam stad** (Rotterdam, 1990)

Casciato, M. et al. (eds.), **Architectuur en volkshuisvesting. Nederland 1870-1940** (Nijmegen, 1980)

Colenbrander, B., **De verstrooide stad** (Rotterdam, 1999) English summary

Crimson, **Re-Urb. Nieuwe plannen voor oude steden** (Rotterdam, 1997)

Damen, H. and A.M. Devolder (eds.), **Lotte Stam-Beese 1902-1988. Dessau, Brno, Charkow, Moskou, Amsterdam, Rotterdam** (Rotterdam, 1993) English summary

Devolder, A. (ed.), **Alexanderpolder. Waar de stad verder gaat/Alexanderpolder. New Urban Frontiers** (Bussum, 1993) Dutch/English

Doevendans, K., J. Luiten and R. Rutgers, **Stadsvorm Tilburg. Stadsontwerp en beeldkwaliteit** (Eindhoven, 1996)

Doevendans, K. and R. Stolzenberg, **De wijkgedachte in Nederland** (Eindhoven, 1988)

Essers, H.A. (ed.), **Stokstraatgebied Maastricht. Een renovatieproces in historisch perspectief** (Maastricht, 1973)

Freijser, V., **Het veranderende stadsbeeld van Den Haag. Plannen en processen in de Haagse stedebouw 1890-1990** (Zwolle, 1991)

Gall, S. (ed.), **Stedebouw in beweging** (Rotterdam, 1993)

Geurts, A.J., **De 'Groene' IJsselmeerpolders. De inrichting van het landschap in Wieringermeer, Noordoostpolder, Oostelijk en Zuidelijk Flevoland** (Lelystad, 1997)

Grinberg, D.I., **Housing in the Netherlands 1900-1940** (Rotterdam, 1977) English

Haan, H. de and I. Haagsma (eds.), **Wie is er bang voor nieuwbouw** (Amsterdam, 1981)

Hacquebord, L.T. and R.M.H. Overbeek, **Architectuur en stedebouw in Groningen 1850-1940** (Zwolle, 1994)

Hellinga, H. et al., **Algemeen Uitbreidingsplan Amsterdam 50 jaar, 1935-1985** (Amsterdam, 1985)

Hoornstra, A. and G. Middelkoop, **De vrije ruimte. Nieuwe strategieën voor de ruimtelijke ordening** (Rotterdam, 1998)

Hoogenberk, E.J., **Het idee van de Hollandse stad. Stedebouw in Nederland 1900-1930 met de internationale voorgeschiedenis** (Delft, 1980)

Hulsbergen, E., V.J. Meyer, M. Paasman, **Stedelijke transformaties. Actuele opgaven in de stad en de rol van de stedebouwkundige discipline** (Delft, 1998)

Idenburg, I., **Zicht op straks. 20.000.000 Nederlanders op 40.000 vierkante kilometers** (Den Haag, 1967, 2^e herziene druk 1971)

Jacobs, K. and L. Smit (eds.), **De ideale stad. Ideaalplannen voor de stad Utrecht 1664-1988** (Utrecht, 1988)

Jong, F. de (ed.), **Stedebouw in Nederland. 50 jaar Bond van Nederlandse Stedebouwkundigen** (Zutphen, 1985)

Kessel, E. van and F. Plastra, **Ir. Jakoba Mulder 1900-1988. Stedebouwkundige en landschapsarchitecte** (Amsterdam, 1994)

Klerk, L.A. de, **Op zoek naar de ideale stad** (Deventer, 1980)

Lambert, A.M., **The making of the Dutch Landscape** (London, 1971) English

Landschap van wegen en kanalen. 75 jaar adviezen van de afdeling Verkeerswegen van het Ministerie van LNV aan de Rijkswaterstaat (Utrecht, 1991)

Lauwen, T. et al., **Nederland als kunstwerk. Vijf eeuwen bouwen door ingenieurs** (Rotterdam, 1995)

Lavooij, W., **Twee eeuwen bouwen aan Arnhem. De stedebouwkundige ontwikkeling van de stad** (Zutphen, 1990)

Lörzing, H., **Van Bosplan tot Floriade. Nederlandse park- en landschapsontwerpen in de twintigste eeuw** (Rotterdam, 1992) English summary

Pasveer, E. (ed.), **Architectuur en stadsvernieuwing** (Delft, 1991)

Reijndorp, A. and M. Nio (eds.), **Groeten uit Zoetermeer. Stedebouw in discussie** (Rotterdam, 1997)

Rikhof, H. and R. Rutgers, **Stadsvorm Tilburg. Historische ontwikkeling** (Eindhoven, 1993)

Rossem, V. van, **Randstad Holland. Variaties op het thema stad** (Rotterdam, 1994)

Ruijter, P., **Voor volkshuisvesting en stedebouw. Voorgeschiedenis, oprichting en programma van het Nederlands Instituut voor volkshuisvesting en stedebouw 1850-1940** (Utrecht, 1987)

Santen, B., **Architectuur en stedebouw in de gemeente Utrecht 1850-1940** (Zwolle, 1990)

Schendelen, M. van, **Natuur en ruimtelijke ordening in Nederland** (Rotterdam, 1997) English summary

Schreijnders, R., **De droom van Howard. Het verleden en de toekomst van de tuindorpen** (Rijswijk, 1991)

Smienk, G. (ed.), **Nederlandse landschapsarchitectuur. Tussen traditie en experiment** (Amsterdam, 1993)

Smook, R.A.F., **Binnensteden veranderen. Atlas van het ruimtelijk veranderingsproces van Nederlandse binnensteden in de laatste anderhalve eeuw** (Zutphen, 1984) English summary

Stichting Rotterdam-Maaskant, **Riek Bakker Ruimte voor Verbeelding** (Rotterdam, 1994)

Taverne, E. and I. Visser (eds.), **Stedebouw: de geschiedenis van de stad in de Nederlanden van 1500 tot heden** (Nijmegen, 1993)

Tummers, L.J.M. and J.M. Tummers, **Het land in de stad. De stedebouw van de grote agglomeratie** (Bussum, 1997) English summary

Valk, A., **Het levenswerk van Th.K. van Lohuizen 1890-1956. De eenheid van het stedebouwkundig werk** (Delft, 1990)

Vreeze, A.S.G. de, **Woningbouw, inspiratie & ambitie. Kwalitatieve grondslagen van de sociale woningbouw in Nederland** (Almere, 1993)

Vreeze, A.S.G. de (ed.), **Orde & chaos in de stadsontwikkeling** (Rotterdam, 1994)

Voorden, F.W. van, **Schakels in stedebouw. Een model voor analyse van de ontwikkeling van de ruimtelijke kwaliteiten van 19de-eeuwse stadsuitbreidingen op grond van een onderzoek in Gelderse steden** (Zutphen, 1983) English summary

Vroom, M.J. (ed.), **Ontwerpen van Nederlandse tuin- en landschapsarchitecten in de periode na 1945/Environments designed by Dutch landscape architects in the period since 1945** (Amsterdam, 1992) Dutch/English

Wal, C. van der, **In Praise of Common Sense: Planning the Ordinary. A Physical Planning History of the New Towns in the IJsselmeerpolders** (Rotterdam, 1997) English

Wit, A. de, **Nieuw Sloten. Van Tuin tot Stad** (Amsterdam, 1998) English summary

Woud, A. van der, **Het Nieuwe Bouwen Internationaal. CIAM Volkshuisvesting, Stedebouw/CIAM Housing, Town Planning** (Delft/Otterlo, 1983) Dutch/English

Index

175

Photocredits

Aerocamera-Michel Hofmeester, Rotterdam 70, 99b, 115, 135t, 152
Aerophoto Eelde 30t, 98
Aeroview - Dick Sellenraad 159b
Algemeen Uitbreidingsplan van Amsterdam. Grondslagen voor de stedebouwkundige ontwikkeling van Amsterdam; deel 1: Nota van toelichtingen, deel 2: Bijlagen (Amsterdam, 1935) 62br
de Architecten cie. / Pi de Bruijn / DRO 171t
de Architecten cie. / Carel Weeber 118t, 144
Archiplan Press, formerly Studio Wim Deppe, Lelystad 135b
Architext 129t
Benthem Crouwel NACO 142b
Bureau Bakker & Bleeker B.V. 140, 141t
Bibliotheek Landbouwuniversiteit, Wageningen 10t
Niek de Boer 88
Boer, N. de & D. Lambert **Woonwijken. Nederlandse stedebouw 1945-1985** (Rotterdam, 1987) 90t
Bouwkundig Weekblad vol.85, 17 (1967) 93t
Blijstra, R., **Nederlandse Stedebouw na 1900** (Amsterdam, n.y.) 75t, 77b, 91t, 101t
Bolles & Wilson Architekten 169t
Van den Broek & Bakema (photo Jan Vrijhof / Netherlands Photo Archives nfa) 93b, 108t
Jo Coenen & Co architekten 146b/m
Tom Croes 129b
Dienst SO Den Haag 76t
DRO VORM fotografie 168t
Ellerman Lucas van Vugt 166b
Eyck, A. van, T.J.J. Bosch, P. de Ley & G. Knemeijer, **Wonen in de binnenstad van Zwolle** (Zwolle, n.y.) 130b
Amsterdam municipal archives 14t, 29
Arnhem municipal archives 11t, 74t
Enschede municipal archives 10b
The Hague municipal archives 11b, 12/13, 61, 76b
Middelburg municipal archives (reproduction Johan Sinke) 71t
Rotterdam municipal archives 35, 43, 71b, 72/73, 92t, 94
Tilburg municipal archives 30b
Utrecht municipal archives (Topographic Historical Atlas) 18, 92b
Zwolle municipal archives 131
Grinberg, D.I., **Housing in the Netherlands 1900-1940** (Rotterdam, 1977) 63t
Groninger Archives 19t, 46t
Michiel Ibelings 15, 25tl, 26, 27, 37, 42, 45b, 63b, 74b, 77t, 83b, 96, 97, 118b, 128t, 134b, 149, 150b
Idenburg, I., **Zicht op straks. 20.000.000 Nederlanders op 40.000 vierkante kilometers** (The Hague, 1967) 110, 111
Katholiek Bouwblad vol.XIV, 22 (1947) 78t
KLM Aerocarto 62t, 119, 148, 163b
Teun Koolhaas Associates 153b
Luuk Kramer 166t, 193t
Hans Krüse / photographic department Delft University of Technology 89
L. Lafour & R. Wijk 145t
MAB Groep B.V. (photo AVEQ) 167
Max. 1 160t
Mecanoo 146, 150t

Mecanoo (photo Christian Richters) 147
MVRDV 159t, 165, 170t
Netherlands Architecture Institute (photo Gerrit Burg) 101b
Netherlands Architecture Institute (reproduction Retina / Martien Kerkhof) 16, 17, 19b, 25tr/b, 26t, 28, 31, 34, 35t, 36t, 44, 45t, 46b, 47, 48, 49, 50, 51, 58, 59, 60, 62lb, 64, 65, 75b, 78b, 79, 80, 82, 83t, 90b, 94t, 99t, 100, 102, 103, 108b, 109, 112, 113, 114, 116t, 120/121, 122, 123, 130t/m, 132, 133, 134t, 145b, 153t
Netherlands Architecture Institute (photo Jan Vrijhof / Netherlands Photo Archives nfa) 91b
Maarten d'Oliviera 33
Office for Metropolitan Architecture OMA 143, 158b, 164bl
Office for Metropolitan Architecture OMA (photo Hans Werlemann) 158t
Cas Oorthuys / Netherlands Photo Archives 57
Philips Company Archives (PCA), Eindhoven 32
Projectbureau Leidsche Rijn, Utrecht 160b
Gert Jan van Rooij 142t
Piet Rook 36t, 128b
J.F.H. Roovers (© H.A. Voet) 95
Peter de Ruig 141b
Ruijter, P., **Voor volkshuisvesting en stedebouw. Voorgeschiedenis, oprichting en programma van het Nederlands Instituut voor volkshuisvesting en stedebouw 1850-1940** (Utrecht, 1987) 19m, 24
Daria Scagliola / Stijn Brakkee 151, 171b
Schie 2.0 164br
Soeters Van Eldonk architecten (photo Martien Kerkhof) 162t
Jaap Swart 116b
Tijdschrift voor Volkshuisvesting en Stedebouw vol.14, 5 (1933) 56
Projectbureau UCP Utrecht Centrum Project 161t
UN Studio Van Berkel & Bos 170b
Ger van der Vlugt 117, 162b
West 8 landscape architects & urban planners b.v. 169b
West 8 landscape architects & urban planners b.v. (photo Jeroen Musch) 168b
René de Wit 161b, 164t
Zanstra, P. et al., **Bouwen, van woning tot stad. Eenige aspecten van den stedebouw, het woningbedrijf, de woningarchitectuur en de technische voorzieningen van de woningen, alsmede van verschillende daarmee samenhangende onderwerpen** (Amsterdam, 1946) 81

Cover
Office for Metropolitan Architecture OMA, Van Berkel & Bos, Christiaanse, Neutelings, West 8, et al. model for Amsterdam Waterfront, development plan for banks of the IJ inlet, Amsterdam (1990-1993)

It was not possible to find all the copyright holders of the illustrations used. Interested parties are requested to contact NAi Publishers, Mauritsweg 23, 3012 JR Rotterdam, the Netherlands.

Colophon

This publication was made possible, in part, by the Netherlands Architecture Fund.

Translation
 Robyn de Jong-Dalziel
Copy editing
 Marianne Lahr
Picture editor
 Ingrid Oosterheerd
Assistance
 Maike Oosterbaan
Graphic design and typesetting
 Lex Reitsma, Haarlem,
 with the assistance of Leon Bloemendaal
Lithography
 Projektiecolor, Hoofddorp
Printing
 Veenman drukkers, Ede
Editing / production
 Caroline Gautier
Publisher
 Simon Franke

Printed and bound in the Netherlands

Available in North, South and Central America through D.A.P. / Distributed Art Publishers, 155 Sixth Avenue, 2nd Floor, New York, NY 10013-1507, Tel. 212 627 1999, Fax 212 627 9484

ISBN 90-5662-085-1